ALSO BY QAZI FAZL ULLAH

Sharia & Politics
Science of Hadith
Hajj and Umrah According to All Four Schools of Jurisprudence
Jihad: Why, How, & When
Sayyidah Aaisha: Age & Marriage
Jesus in the Quran

RAMADAN: COMPONENTS OF THE HOLY MONTH

RAMADAN: COMPONENTS OF THE HOLY MONTH
WRITTEN BY **QAZI FAZL ULLAH**
EDITED BY **EVELYN THOMPSON**

HUND INTERNATIONAL PUBLISHING

LOS ANGELES, CALIFORNIA

2018

COPYRIGHT © 2018 BY QAZI FAZL ULLAH

All rights reserved. This book or any portion thereof may not be reproduced or used in any manner whatsoever without the express written permission of the publisher except for the use of brief quotations in a book review or scholarly journal.

FIRST PRINTING: 2018

ISBN: 978-1-73260-175-8

HUND INTERNATIONAL PUBLISHING

LOS ANGELES, CALIFORNIA

PRINTED IN THE UNITED STATES OF AMERICA

TABLE OF CONTENTS

PREFACE 9

INTRODUCTION 11

MOON SIGHTING 18

ASTRONOMY 23

CONJUCTION AND NEW MOON OR *QIRAN* AND *MUHAQ* 28

WHAT IS *HILAL*? 32

RAMADAN AND SIGHTING 33

ANALYSIS OF THESE *AHADITH* 39

FASTING IN *ISLAM* 42

ADVANTAGES OF FASTING 43

HOW *RAMADAN* STARTS 46

CONDITIONS FOR FASTING 47

WHAT IS RECOMMENDED IN FASTING 48

DISCOURAGED PRACTICES DURING FASTING 50

ACCEPTABLE EXCUSES NOT TO FAST OR BREAK A FAST 51

QADA IN FASTING 53

THINGS THAT DO NOT BREAK THE FAST 55

TARAWEEH 56

ITIKAF (SECLUSION) 57

VIRTUES OF *RAMADAN*	58
LAILAT UL QADR & *EID UL FITR*	60
IMPORTANCE AND VIRTUES OF *RAMADAN*	61
PHILOSOPHY OF FASTING	64
SALAT UL TARAWEEH	66
HOW *PROPHET MUHAMMAD* PERFORMED *QIYAM*	73
TARAWEEH IN THE TIME OF *KHULAFAH-I-RASHIDIN*	82
TABI'EEN	89
THE PRACTICE OF JURISTS	92
THE PRACTICE OF THE FOUR *IMAMS*	95
SALAT UL WITR	97
HOW MANY *RAKAT* IS THIS?	104
TA'AMULUS - SAHABAH WAT - TABIEEN	112
THE *RIWAYAAT* AND ANALYSIS	117
HOW TO PRAY THESE THREE *RAKAT*	126
WHAT IS *ITIKAF*?	134
ZAKAT	137
IMPORTANT ISSUES IN *ZAKAT*	139
BOOKS BY *QAZI FAZL ULLAH*	145
ABOUT THE AUTHOR	159

PREFACE

Praise be to *Allah* (*Subhanahu Wa Ta'ala*) and Peace and Blessings be upon His Beloved *Prophet*, *Muhammad* (Peace Be Upon Him), his companions, family and followers.

Islam as a *Deen* is perfect and complete,

as *Allah* said:

> *"This day, I have perfected for you your Deen (5:3)."*

The approach of this *Deen* is very reasonable and logical. *Allah* intends ease for us. It addressees the general public, which is why the common layman was taken into consideration when making its rules.

A *Muslim* is bound to obey *Allah* and His Messenger to the best of his ability. That is the ultimate achievement.

> *"And whosoever obeys Allah and His Messenger, so indeed, he has achieved a great success (33:70)."*

Islam has five pillars of faith, and the third one after declaration of *Tauheed* and *Risalat* and is *Saum*, which is fasting during *Ramadan*.

Ramadan is the ninth month of *Islamic* calendar, which is lunar-based. The start of an *Islamic* lunar month is based upon the moon when it becomes totally dark at the time of conjunction, or a new moon when it comes very close to sun, which is called moon birth, or when it goes on a specific distance from the sun towards east and it is seen for the first time at the time of sunset, which is called *Hilal* (crescent).

This book is written to clarify the concepts and maintain them as they have been since the time of the *Prophet Muhammad*. May *Allah* accept this effort! *Amin*!

INTRODUCTION

Islam is based upon five pillars. These pillars are to keep the structure of faith standing over one to establish a relationship and connection with *Allah*.

As this is the way to establish your connection to *Allah*, so His injunctions may be followed in both word and deed so that one may not go astray, except the very first pillar, which is the declaration of *Islam*, or *Kalimah* and *Shahadah*, and does not have any time specification. The other four pillars have their time either fixed by *Shariah* itself, like prayer, fasting and *Hajj* (pilgrimage to *Mecca*), or a *Muslim* has an option to fix his own time for it i.e., any day of a lunar month, but once he fixed it, then that will be the fixed date, and this is in the case of *Zakat* (tithing to the poor).

Regarding prayer, *Allah* said:

> *"Indeed, prayer is mandatory for believers in its appointed time (4:103)."*

Also, *Allah* said:

> *"Keep up prayer from the declining of the sun till the darkness of the night and the morning recitation (Fajr Prayer). Surely, the mornings recitation is witnessed (by the angels) (17:78)."*

Prayer in *Islam* is five times a day. *Islam* has fixed its times based upon the sun and upon the alternation of day and night. Angel *Jibril* (known as Gabriel in the West) came to the *Prophet* for two days and led him in five prayers: the first day in the starting time of every prayer and the second day in the ending time of every prayer and said,

> *"These are the times of prayer for you and your Ummah."*

The sun's rise and set determine the times of prayer. The breaking of dawn and the falling of twilight (*Shafaq*) are also signs. But for *Hajj*, *Zakat* and fasting, the moon is made a sign to fix its time to perform. These three are to be performed once a year in a specific month, and the month is to be known by the appropriate phase of the moon. Some people asked the *Prophet* about it:

> *They ask you about crescents (it appears, then waxes, then becomes full, then wanes, then disappears. Why?) Tell (them): "These are signs for people and for Hajj and this is not righteousness to enter the houses from its back. But righteous is one who kept his duty (to Allah) and came to the houses from its doors, and keep up your duty (to Allah,) so you may get into success (2:189)."*

This verse made it clear that the original sign to determine the months is the moon and not the sun, because the solar year is not a natural year, but based upon astronomical calculations, while the lunar year is natural, as the moon completes its course and cuts all 12 mansions and 28 steps in one month only, and repeats the same course 12 times a year, while the sun completes it only once a year.

Allah said:

> *"Verily the number of months near Allah is 12 months in Allah's ordinance since that He [Allah created the heavens and the earth. Of these, four [months] are sacred. This is an established system, so be not unjust to yourselves regarding them (9:36)."*

Regarding verse 2:189, it is said that after *Hajj* the people of the peninsula used to enter their houses not through the front entrances but from the back, as they were of the view that when we are washed of our sins, so we may change our entrance as well, at least for our first entering to our houses after that wash. Maybe this was their custom and their faith as well, but to make this part of the *Ayah* (rules/signs) related to the issue of crescents, they asked about it. It is said that as they asked the *Prophet* about an astronomical issue, so *Allah* said, asking an astronomical issue from the *Prophet* is as wrong as entering to the house from the back, forsaking the proper entrance. He may have asked the *Shariah*, and then *Allah* answered the question, in a way that made the *Islamic* issue clear regarding crescents.

Now, it is clear that calendar is of 12 months, either solar or lunar, and the sun and moon are the two signs for this respectively. They both travel in an orbit (*Falak*).

For their traverse the astronomers said that there are 12 invisible mansions in the orbit.

Allah said:

> *By the heaven, having Buruj (mansions), [this word also means big stars or planets as well].*

Allah also said:

> *And the moon we have measured it in mansions [stages].*

Also, He (*Allah*) said:

> *"This is not for the sun to overtake the moon, nor can the night overtake the day, each one floats in an orbit (36:40)."*

These verses made it clear that the sun and moon both travel in their orbits in an orderly fashion. Therefore, *Allah* made the sun a sign for day and night and the moon for months and years. That is why for prayer, the sun is used, and its turning times are fixed, and for other worships the moon and its changes are used. In this regard, we quote a few verses of the *Holy Qur'an*:

> *"And he subjected the sun and the moon (to an established system) each one runs (its course) for a term appointed. He (Allah) manages/regulates all affairs. He explains the Ayat (rules/signs) that you may believe with certainty in the Meeting with your Lord (13:2)."*

> *"(He,) is the cleaver of the daybreak. He has appointed the night for resting and the sun and the moon for reckoning/calculation. This is the determination of the All-Mighty, the All-Knower (6:96)."*

> *"The sun and the moon run on their fixed courses (for calculation/on precise calculation.) (55:5)."*

The word *Husban* is from *Hisab*, which means calculation – so it means that both sun and moon run on calculation and for calculation –

> *"on calculation"*

mean that both run on a precise calculation making no deviations and are never disturbed,

as *Allah* said:

> *"And the sun runs on its course for a term appointed/towards a place appointed. This is the determination of the All-Mighty, All-Knower, and for the moon We have appointed mansions/stages till it becomes like a dried old date palm trees branch [i.e., curved]. It is not for the sun to reach/overtake the moon, nor for the night to outstrip the day. They all float each in an orbit (36:38-40)."*

Or *Husban* means

> *"for calculation,"*

so these are the means of calculation,

as *Allah* said:

> *"He is the One Who made the sun a shining light and the moon a derived light and determined for it [the moon] stages so you may know the computation of years and*

reckoning Allah has not created that but in Truth. He details the signs/rules for the people who know (10:5)."

In this verse the pronoun "His" in "Qaddarahu" is towards the moon as the moon's floating through its stages is quick and the months and years are known through that. While the months meant in "Shariah" are the lunar months and the year meant there is also the lunar year and not the solar one and the stages for moon are 28 stages, as every mansion has 2 and 1/3 stages and the moon goes through one stage every night till it passes these 28 stages, then it disappears (could not be seen from the earth) for two nights if the month is of thirty days and disappears for one night if that is of twenty-nine (Tafsir I Khazin, Volume 2).

Many *Mufasireen* mention the same thing.

The moon disappears in the end of every month as we mentioned and that is called *Muhaq, Imtihaq, Qiran Ush Shamsi Wal Qamar* or *Ijtima Al Munirain* in *Arabic*, while the astronomers call it new moon, or conjunction.

An eclipse happens when the earth, moon and the sun all fall in one straight line, then that face of the moon that is towards the earth cannot be seen, as no sunlight of sun falls on that face in the time of *Muhaq* (darkness) or that new Moon in that Conjunction time could not be seen from the earth. It does not mean that the moon is gone. It is simply not visible from earth. It stays that way for a night or two at the most, so logically it could not be used to prove something. But the source should be something proven, known or seen, and this proof should be attainable for common people. For this reason, the proof is when the moon becomes a crescent, i.e., when a part of it becomes bright and visible.

Allah said:

> *"By the sun and its brightness/brilliance. By the moon when it follows it (91:1-2)."*

It means the *Muhaq* or conjunction, as the moon follows the sun, falling in one and the same straight line with the sun and the earth, and follows the sunset, with no considerable time between sunset and moonset. It can mean when it follows the sun, by being a distance from the sun, and follows the sunset by a considerable interval afterwards.

MOON SIGHTING

HOW CAN A NEW MOON BE DETERMINED *ISLAMICALLY*?

As we mentioned before the verse of *Surat Ul Baqarah* (2:189) where *Allah* made it clear that *Hilal*, the crescent, is the source and sign for time fixing, the same concept is further elaborated by various *Ahadith* (sayings) of the *Prophet*, where their sighting is mentioned regarding the beginning of a new month, which we will mention later. But here we should find out the philosophy of this time fixing in general.

1. The time fixing for various worship via the sun or moon is for establishing a relationship between nature and *Sharia*, as everything in this world including the sun and moon prostrate to *Allah*,

   as He said:

   "See you not (O Muhammad) that Allah, He it is Whom glorify whatsoever is in the heaven and the earth and Allah is All-Aware of what they do (24:41)."

> *"Whatsoever is in the heavens and whatsoever is on the earth glorifies Allah (61:1)."*
>
> *"And to Allah prostrate whatsoever is there in the heavens and whatsoever is in on the earth (16:49)."*
>
> *"See you not that whatsoever is in the heaven and whatsoever is on the earth, the sun, the moon, the stars, the mountains, the trees, the living moving creatures and many of the mankind prostrate to Allah, but there are many (men) on whom the punishment is justified, and whomsoever Allah disgraces, none can honor him. Verily, Allah does what He wills (22:18)."*

The prostration of nature to *Allah* and its praise to Him means fulfillment of the natural duties as determined by *Allah*, so when human beings fulfill their religious duties to *Allah* at prescribed times, it creates a resemblance between nature and *Shariah* in fulfillment of their respective duties. This is the time that makes people addressees of the commandments concerned from time to time as this Commandment is repeated automatically with the coming of the time fixed for the same. So even though the basic cause for any worship is the order of *Allah*, the time fixed is also a cause and reason for that timing, so whenever the cause repeats the worship repeats along with it, as this is detailed in jurisprudence.

2. In such a fixing there is simplicity that is the very nature of this natural religion.

Allah said:

"So set you your face towards the religion with full sincerity, [be committed to] Allah's nature with which He has created the mankind. No change let there be in the creation/nature [religion] of Allah. This is the straight/established religion, but most people know not (30:30)."

The *Prophet* said:

"My Ummah (people) will be on (follow) nature/natural system forever."

This means

"news,"

or even an order by the *Prophet* not to go against the nature.

3. The base of this religion is ease as *Allah* said:

   "Allah wants for you the ease and He does not want hardship for you (2:185)."

   "Allah does not make one bound but to the extent of his power (2:186)."

   "We do not make one bound but to the extent of his power (6:152/7:42/23:62)."

   "Allah wants to lighten (the burden) for you and man is created weak (4:28)."

> *"No person shall have a burden laid on him greater than he can bear (2:233)."*
>
> *"And He has not laid down upon you in religion any hardship (22:78)."*

There are several other verses of the *Holy Quran* in this regard. *Abu Huraira* narrates that the *Prophet* said:

> *"Religion is very easy and whoever overburdens himself in his religion will not be able to continue in that way. So you should not be extremists, but try to be near to perfection and receive the good tidings so you may be rewarded and gain strength by offering the (prayer) in the mornings, afternoons and during the last hours of the nights (Bukhari Volume 1)."*

For the said purpose of simplicity and ease, *Allah* made the sun, its movements, and the changing of the day and night as markers for prayer, and the moon for other worships.

4. Diversities

Mankind likes diversities in prayer by nature. They satisfy this taste for diversity by praying at different times, while arranging annual worships it so that they fall in different seasons due to the shift of the lunar calendar, and that gives it a new taste.

5. Universal Equality

People in different areas perform the same in different seasons. For example, if people in Asia are fasting in summer, at the same time it is winter in Australia, and vice-versa. This is equality and Justice as well.

Now, before we proceed to analyze the *Ayat* and *Ahadith* regarding moon sighting, we want to talk a little bit about astronomy, which is not the only source in *Shariah*, but neither it is ignored totally.

ASTRONOMY

Under *Islamic Sharia*, belief in astrology is unlawful, as astrology attributes destiny, good and bad luck, and news about the future of individuals, to the heavenly bodies. Astronomy, however, is totally a different field.

It has three branches:

A. The study of the physical structure of the heaven and heavenly bodies and its nature.

B. The study of the movements of these heavenly bodies and calculations thereof.

C. The crafting and refining of the tools/apparatus and utensils for movements and calculation.

To know, learn, and study astronomy is a collective responsibility of the *Ummah* as it can be used for certain religious issues, like prayer times, direction of the *Qibla*, timings of solar or lunar eclipses, moon sightings, etc. That is why *Ali* said that knowing about astronomy will strengthen the faith of the person concerned; and *Ibni Abbas* said that this is a part of the knowledge given to the *Prophets,* which means it was of divine origin. Also, it is said that the first one who dealt with this field was *Prophet Idris* (Enoch). He laid down its basic rules and tenets. *Maimun Ibni Mehran* also said that this is a part of the divine knowledge. In the biography of *Imam Malik*, it is said that he wrote a book on astronomy.

Taqi Ud Din Sabuki wrote:

> *"For moon sighting it is a must that the* qadi *[decisive authority] may know astronomy himself or at least to ask about it from the people who know about this (Al-Ilmul Manthur) so he may accept or reject the testimony about moon sighting as he will be already aware of the possibility of moon sighting, because if there is no possibility, then how someone has seen it."*

Ibni Aud writes:

> *"If the proper calculation say that sighting is impossible, then the testimony may be rejected as in testimony the possibility is the first-ever condition (Minhat Ul Ali Il Muta 'al, p.72)."*

Also, he quoted from the Book of *Hafiz Ibni Hajar*:

> *...And the testimony of the witnesses may be rejected when it contradicts the certain calculation (p.12).*

This testimony regarding sighting is like all other testimonies in its acceptance and rejection. Even for the acceptance of the narration of *Hadith* there are conditions as *Ibni Hajar* said:

> *And from these [reasons of rejection] is the position of the narrated Hadith as if its contradicts the text of Qur'an or a Matawatur Hadith [narrated by few just, authentic narrators] or contradicts* ijma *[consensus of Jurists] or contradicts a sound intellect (Nukhbatal Fikar)."*

Hafiz Ibni Jawzi said:

> *Every Hadith you find against sound intellects or that contradicts the (sound authentic) principles, then know that is fabricated/false or if the sense, vision and sight rejects the same, or that goes against the text of the Book or against "Sunnat I Mutwatirah" or Ijma' (Fathul-Mughith, p.114).*

In the *Holy Qur'an*, *Allah* said that one who makes false charges of adultery or fornication against someone and that falsification is proven in court, his testimony may not be accepted as his personality is marred and his credibility is lost. Conversely, that testimony would be accepted when no doubt is there, neither in the person, nor in his statement, nor in the very thing he testifies about.

Prophet Idris (Enoch) introduced astronomy as a subject and knowledge. The *Prophets* take their knowledge through inspiration from *Allah*, so this is a divine knowledge as well.

Allama Aulusi, the *Mufassir*, said:

> *For example, if it is said that this coming month the Hilal could be sighted when it will be on a distance of 12 degrees and 20 minutes and at that time it could be seen near 40 degrees' longitude at sunset time. This longitude*

is Saudi Arabia, so it could be seen and it will become further bright when it proceeds to the west, so we will say that the Hilal of such-and-such month was seen near 40 degrees' longitude area.

Matale (sighting points) change every month because the rotation of the moon around the earth is not fixed forever. Yes, its average is 27 days, 7 hours, 43 minutes, and 6 or 11 seconds. Yes, the time between two new moons is 29.5 days but these are averages and approximations. There these extra two days are also needed for the moon to appear as a *Hilal* and that is why the lunar month is sometimes 29 days and sometimes 30 days, and because of this average of 29.5 plus days in 30 lunar years, 11 eleven years are leap years, where *Zul Hijja* is of 30 days, like the leap month of February in every fourth solar year, because the average solar year is 365.25 days.

The moon rotates around the earth 12 times in one lunar year and 8.33 extra time remains and that is why in 30 years there are eleven leap years.

The time between the new moon and its becoming *Hilal* differ in different months because the moon's orbit differs by day as well, in between 12 degrees and 15.25 degrees and that's why the *Matale* change as well, and the earth could not be zoned on permanent basis as far as sighting and *Matale* is concerned.

The moon completes its course around the earth in 29 days, 12 hours, 44 minutes, 2.9 seconds. This calculation is accurate and was instrumental in the moon landing. As the moon's surface is not flat but spherical and there are hills and caves which obstruct the sunlight on t the moon's surface, and the moon will reflect it, so when the light of the sun goes up then these hills and a part of moon reflects it, that is *Hilal*.

The new moon cannot be seen from anywhere without the use of strong binoculars. This new moon passes in between the earth and the sun every month, but when it comes right down the middle and blocks the sun, the result is a solar eclipse. This eclipse only happens at the time of the new moon and lasts a short time.

The time between the new moon and *Hilal* differ. It could be 15-17 hours, and up to 32 hours. Normally a *Hilal* about 22-24 hours old can be seen with the naked eye.

For sighting, a combination of a few things is needed like the age of the moon, the distance, and the time after sunset. For sighting purposes, the distance should be as the earth can cut 10.5 degrees, it cuts one degree in 4 minutes. Also, the rising point of the moon is another factor.

This is not prohibited to study astronomy in depth to know the times for prayers, the direction of *Qibla*, and solar and lunar eclipses, but some parts of it is *Fardi Kifayah*, and *Ali* said:

> *"The scholar of Qur'an, if he studies the astronomy, it will strengthen His belief."*

CONJUCTION AND NEW MOON OR *QIRAN* AND *MUHAQ*

"CONJUNCTION" AND *"NEW MOON"* OR *QIRAN* AND *MUHAQ*

As we said when the sun, the earth, and the moon are straight in the same line and the moon is not seen to the people on the earth, that is called conjunction, or *Muhaq*. After *Qiran* or *Muhaq*, when a part of it becomes bright for the first time and is seen to the people at sunset time that is called *Hilal* or crescent, and that is the base of *Islamic* calculation.

Then this brightness spreads slowly on moon's surface, till it becomes fully bright and that is called the full moon. After that once again its brightness decreases till it disappears and that is

"Conjunction."

The moon from one conjunction time to the next time is called a

"real lunar month."

This time differs in different months from 29 days and 5 hours to 29 days and 19 hours. This month starts anytime of the day and night because when the conjunction takes place that will be during the day somewhere and night at another place. But in *Islam* the next month starts with the sighting and ends with the sighting of the next month. This month is sometimes 29 days and sometimes 30 days.

For the sun and moon's traverses, astronomers, *Muslims* and non-*Muslims*, alike, have fixed 12 mansions in the orbit. The sun completes its traverse in all these mansions in 12 months, while the moon completes it in one month. Both bodies orbit their axes in 24 hours. The moon itself is not bright, but it reflects the sunlight.

THE CONJUNCTION TIME TAKES PLACE ALL OVER THE WORLD, BUT FOR HOW LONG DOES IT STAND UNSEEN?

To answer this question, we quote the sayings of astronomers that for sighting the moon must get out of the light of the sun to reflect to such an extent that we can see it.

BUT HOW MUCH SHOULD THIS DISTANCE BE?

The answer is that at the time of sunset it should be at least 8 degrees from the sun towards east. Some others said it should be on a distance of 10 degrees. A third saying is that it should be on a distance of 12 or 13 degrees, and nobody said more than 13 degrees that it is needed. Another saying is that it should stand still for 40 minutes after sunset to be seen. Now if we will take the saying of 12 degrees into consideration, then it means it should stand unseen for 24 degrees, that is, 12 degrees towards west of the sun, then 12 degrees towards east of it to be seen.

Then the moon cuts one degree in two hours at the most, so it means it will stand unseen for 48 hours as it will be to the sun's west for 24 hours and then towards its east for another 24 hours to be seen, and when it cuts the 12 degrees to sun's west and comes very close to the sun that is called a new moon. After this again it goes on a distance from the sun, but to its east till it appears and seen and that is called *Hilal*.

Now as the sayings are different, that is why based on the saying of 8 degrees this unseen time will be 32 hours, and based on 10 degrees' saying it could be 40 hours. Thus, the crescent could be seen 20 to 22 hours after conjunction, but there are still different opinions based on observations and experience. The most famous opinion is that of 24 hours, but this is based upon probability.

Now regarding an eclipse, conjunction and the new moon the calculation is an accurate thing, but it is not as accurate with regards to sighting.

The sighting can never be at the same time or the same day every year, as there is an invisible separation on the earth so the same day the moon could not be sighted to the east of the separation. But to its west it may be seen. This separator is hundreds of miles in the middle of the globe from east to west. But from north to south, it includes almost half of the globe. This separator happens every month on different parts of the globe. So, every month the sighting to the east of that separator is impossible to its west. To its west it would be seen, while in between it is possible to be sighted.

Once it is seen in a place, then to the west of that place it could be sighted for sure, but not everywhere, but rather in different parts as the rotation of the earth and its global shape are the affecting factors in this regard, and that is why *Hilal* cannot be sighted at the same time in the same zone even.

New moon is in a time when the sun and the moon both are on the same degree of the zodiac, i.e., they are as much close to each other as possible. Then the moon goes to the east of the sun, and it that is at a distance of 12 degrees from the sun it could be seen and that is *Hilal* as we said before, but there are certain other factors also, so astronomically it cannot be said exactly that it must be seen at such-and-such a place, because its distance is 12 degrees. Sometimes it can be seen a little before that distance, while sometimes it needs a little bit more time after 12 degrees to be seen.

To pinpoint the place or movements of heavenly bodies, the same longitude and latitude theory applies to the space as is applied to the earth.

WHAT IS *HILAL*?

This is derived from *Ahalla*, which means *Zahara*, so *Hilal* means the moon that has appeared. Then the appearance is the first one, which is why the first night's moon is called *Hilal*. Its plural is *Ahillah*, which is mentioned in the *Ayah* of *Surat Ul Baqarah*, but in *Ahadith* this singular is used.

RAMADAN AND SIGHTING

Allah said:

"O you who believe! Fasting is prescribed for you as it was prescribed for those before you so you may become pious, for a fixed number of days, but if any of you is ill or on a journey, the same number [should be fasted] from other days. And as for those who can fast with difficulty they have to feed a poor one [for each day], but whoever does good of his own accord, it is better for him, and that you fast it is better for you if only you knew. The month of Ramadan is that in which was revealed the Qur'an as guidance for people and clear rules of guidance and the criterion, so whoever of you sight the Shahr [Crescent] he must fast it and whoever is ill or traveling, so the same number of days (he may fast) from other days (2:183-184)."

In these verses there are a few important points regarding sighting which is our subject here.

"Fa man Shahida min Kumush'shahra, Fal Yasumhu"

Here there are two words:

Shahida and *Shahr*.

All *Ahadith* regarding moon sightings are in the Juristic explanation of this verse, as *Shahida* is from *Shuhud*, which means observation. So, if the object of *Shuhud* is a place, then it means who attended the place or found it, and if its object is an event or a thing then it means observed.

Now in the above verse, the object is *Shahr* and that is time, so some jurists said that here *Shahida* means *Hadara* and that means *Adraka* i.e., so whosoever found the *Shahr* (time). But it does not work as with the verb *Hadara*; the time may be a subject and not an object or the time may be used as genitive *(Majroor)* with *fi*, so it should have been either

"Faman Shahidahush Shahru"

so to whom the month (time) came or

"Faman Shahida Fish-Shahr"

so whosoever attended the month while the time is already mentioned in the previous verses 183 and 184

"Kutiba Alaikumus Siyamu" – Ayyamam Madudat."

Fasting is prescribed for you for a fixed number of days and later it is made further clear in *Ayat* 185 where *Allah* said,

"Shahru Ramadan."

So, there was no need of another sentence.

Some scholars said that *Shahida* is in the meaning of *Adraka*, so whosoever from amongst you found the month while some others said it means whosoever was in the city in the month means he was not traveling, so he may fast. But in such a way you must put a few *Muqaddarat* (hidden but implied words) and to be in city is the normal situation of everyone, while traveling happens.

Then some others said that *Shahida* means *Aayana* or *Ra'aa* and *Shahr* means *Hilal* (crescent) and not month.

So, the verse means,

"*whosoever saw the crescent,*"

and the crescent is that which is seen for the first time after conjunction.

Then *Ramadan* is mentioned after this to make clear that *Ramadan* is based upon *Hilal* and the *Hilal* mostly appears on the 29th of every month and *Muslims* are bound to look for it. This is *Fardi Kifayah* and sometimes it appears on 30th, but the *Qur'an* did not mention *Ra'aa* but *Aayana*, which is more inclusive.

Then this sentence is *Shartiya*, which means

"*and whosoever saw and testified this must fast.*"

In *Arabic*, this type of sentence means the opposite, which means

"*and if nobody saw and testified then do not fast.*"

Also, the sentence says,

"if whosoever amongst you saw..."

which means it is not a must that everyone needs to see and testify. Also, some people will see that on one day in a certain place and some others will see it the other day in another place. It indicates *Ikhtilaful Matale*.

Also, it did not say

"Fa In Shahida"

meaning

"if someone..."

or

"Fa Iza Shahida...", when someone saw....",

so the verse made it clear that *Shuhud* is the base of the decision about the month's start, so *Shuhud* will make fasting *Fard*, and if not, then there is no fasting.

Ramadan is the time for fasting. But *Ramadan* is based upon *Shuhud*. *Hajj* also depends upon *Shuhud*. But it is not mentioned there because *Ramadan's* time to start it is very strict, so disputes can happen.

In this regard there are a few *Ahadith*, but we will take a few of them to analyze it, as the others we lift are of the same meaning.

> *Ibni Umar relates from the Prophet that Allah has made the crescents Mawaqeet [the signs for months] so when you saw it then start fasting and when you saw it then do*

Fitr. And if became ambiguous for you then calculate it i.e., 30 days (Ahmad, Hakim, Bayhaqi).

Ibni Umar narrated from the Prophet we are illiterate community, we cannot write nor we can calculate, month is like this, this and this (i.e., sometime 29 days and sometime 30 days) (Bukhari, Muslim, Abu Dawud, Ahmad, Nisa'i).

Abu Huraira narrated from the Prophet that month will be 29 days while sometimes it will be 30 days, so when you saw it, start fasting and when you saw it then do Fitr. If it became ambiguous then complete the number (of 30 days) (Abu Dawud, Nisa'i).

Ibni Umar said from the Prophet that he mentioned Ramadan So he said, "Do not start fasting until you see the Crescent and do not do Fitr *till you see it. If it was ambiguous to you then calculate it (Bukhari, Muslim).*

Abdur Rahman Ibni Zaid Ibnul Khattab said from the Prophet that fast for sighting and do Fitr for sighting and do Nask (qurbani and Hajj) for it and if it became ambiguous for you then complete 30 and if two witnesses testified then do fast and do Fitr (Nisa'i).

Ibni Abbas said from the Prophet not to fast before Ramadan.

Fast for it is sighting and do Fitr for it is sighting and if there became any ambiguity in front of it then complete 30 days (Tirmizi).

Abu Huraira relates that the Prophet said not to go ahead of Ramadan by one day or two days, but if a person used to fast a day so he may do it (Tirmizi).

Kuraib says that Ummah Fadl Bintal Harith sent him to Mua'wiyah in Sham. He says I came to Sham and accomplished her need and the Hilal of Ramadan was announced on me in Sham so we saw Hilal on Friday night, then I came to Medina in the ending days of the month, so Abdullah Ibni Abbas asked me, then he mentioned the Hilal. He said; when you did you see it? I said, we saw it Friday night. He asked me, have you seen it? I said "yes", and the people also saw it and they fasted and Mua'wiyah as well. Then he [Ibni Abbas] said but we saw it Saturday night, so we will be going on fasting till we complete 30 days or we see it. So, I said you are not ok with the sighting of Mua'wiyah and his fasting. He said, "No [that is not the case]." This way the Prophet ordered us to do (Ahmad, Muslim, Abu Dawud, Tirmizi, Nisa'i).

ANALYSIS OF THESE *AHADITH*

In the first *Hadith* by *Ibni Umar* it is mentioned that crescents are the *Mawaqeet* for the start of month everywhere for every people in every month.

In the verse of *Holy Qur'an*, the same thing is mentioned and their *Hajj* is mentioned to give a due attention to it that *Hajj* is performed in a specific month and that is also based upon moon sighting.

Also, in this *Hadith* it is said that sighting is the first ever thing in this regard, while number and count is the last resort.

The second *Hadith* of *Ibni Umar* in which it is said

"we are illiterate"

is to make it clear that *Deen* may not be made complicated, but are to be kept very simple so that the common people may understand them and execute them correctly.

The *Hadith* of *Abu Hurairah* says that the 29th day of every month is the day on which the sighting must be attempted.

The *Hadith* of *Ibni Umar* that says,

> *"don't fast till you see the Hilal,"*

which means not to fast without sighting, and the *Hadith* of *Ibni Abbas* supports it, saying, do not go ahead of *Ramadan* by one or two days. Also, a legal maxim said, wherever there is a condition for something and the condition does not happen, the conditioned thing will not happen as well; in other words, when there is no sighting, there can be no fasting.

The *Hadith* of *Abdur Rahman* said if two witnesses testify, then do fasting. Here the *Hadith* of *Kuraib* is very clear in *Ikhtilaful Matale* and *Ibni Abbas* confirmed that this concept is taken from the *Prophet*.

So *Ikhtilaful Matale* is logical, practical, observed, and reasonable, and mentioned in the text in one way or the other, because *Shuhud* is condition and in these *Ahadith* it is clearly stated that when a sighting is proven, the fasting is confirmed as well, and practical sighting in different places will schedule the fasting for different days. But *Imam Jassas* said that this sighting is not specific for people of that specific area, so when it is proven in one place, that is for all places. But we say one is the order of sighting, that is universal; second is to take into consideration the zone in question, otherwise if we will take into consideration the generality of the verse

> *"Perform the prayer"*

with the decline of the sun, then when the decline takes place in far east, the people all over the world may pray *Zuhr*, and this is illogical.

SO, WE SAY THE ORDER IS GENERAL, BUT WHEN DOES IT APPLY?

Islam specifies, the *Sabab* (cause) for every practice, and when that cause exists, then that practice may be done. So, it is not reasonable for the cause to happen in one zone and the practice to be required in another zone.

In the case of moon sighting, astronomers' calculations may be taken into consideration to accept the witnesses' claims or to reject them.

WHAT IS THE CRITERION FOR *IKHTILAFUL MATALE*?

Imam Wali Ullah and *Imam Nawawi* said it should be the distance of *Shari Safar*. One state under one authority is one *Matla*. There are few other opinions as well, but the best one is if the difference between two places is the difference of day and night, or those places share the night can be considered one *Matla*. In cloudy weather where sighting is not possible, residents should follow sighting of the moon in the nearest clear sky.

FASTING IN *ISLAM*

Fasting during the month of *Ramadan* is one of the five pillars of *Islam*. It is mandatory for every *Muslim* adult, male or female, who do not possess an allowable excuse to abstain. Fasting is a common practice in many religions, although there are differences in the nature and timing of the fasts. Fasting in *Islam* became an obligation on *Sha'ban* 10th in the second year after *Hijra*, and after the change in *Qibla* from *Baitul Maqdas* to *Baitullah*.

ADVANTAGES OF FASTING

THE ADVANTAGES OF FASTING ARE:

1. Definition of fasting: Fasting is defined by the jurists to

   "Abstain from three things; eating, drinking, and sexual pleasure, for the entire day when there is an intention of fasting."

2. Wisdom and philosophy: The basic philosophy behind any commandment and prohibition is obedience and submission, for that is the meaning of *Islam*. But every prescribed action in *Islam* also has an underlying philosophy and certain advantages. The advantages of fasting are:

a) It establishes discipline and further enhances a person's strength of will, patience, and stability.

b) It instills a sense of equality within *Muslims* across all economic stratifications, for every *Muslim* adult is bound to fast, in the same way, regardless of whether they are rich or poor.

c) It strengthens a *Muslims* belief in *Allah* by abstaining from food and drink, even in solitude, reinforcing the belief that *Allah* is All-Seeing and All-Hearing.

d) It regulates and disciplines our schedule of eating and drinking.

e) It instills a sense of empathy and compassion for other *Muslims*, for it allows us to feel the pain of deprivation, hunger and thirst experienced by people in need.

f) It teaches self-control against our own physical lusts and desires.

g) It is a means for promoting mental peace, relaxation, and satisfaction.

h) The regulation of food intake during fasting has tremendous physical benefits to the body; after a month of fasting the body feels invigorated, renewed and energized.

i) It teaches one how to face adversity and hardships.

As *Rasoolullah (Prophet Muhammad)* said,

"Fasting is a shield."

He also said,

"One who fasted and prayed during the night in the month of Ramadan with stern belief and with full sincerity, his past sins are pardoned."

In another *Hadith* it is said,

"Fasting in Ramadan wipes out small sins when one avoids the major sins."

HOW *RAMADAN* STARTS

Islamic calendar and *Islamic* rules pertaining to dates are based upon the lunar calendar. The start of a lunar month is based upon the sighting of the moon, or when 30 days have elapsed since the start of the previous month. Regarding moon sightings, we need a testamentary statement from two just *Muslims* or at least one just, honest, integrated *Muslim*. But the possibility of sighting according to astronomers is a pre-requisite. When the moon is sighted in one region, it is deemed sufficient for all people located to the west of that region, provided that the *Qazi* or *Waali* of the *Muslims* endorses that decision. The age of the moon, and consequently its brightness and size, will increase for all areas lying westward from any given location where the initial sighting took place.

CONDITIONS FOR FASTING

The basic conditions for fasting are: *Islam*, intention, puberty, sanity, and capability. Capability implies being of health and for women not to be menstruating or bleeding following childbirth. Regarding intention, *Imam Shafi* and *Imam Ahmed* said that it must be made at night before the break of dawn every single day. *Imam Malik* says that it may be made during the night but also it is allowed until before sunset every day. *Imam Abu Hanifa* takes a very logical view and has said that as *Ramadan* is one single unit, so the intention once at the beginning of *Ramadan* is enough for the entire month.

WHAT IS RECOMMENDED IN FASTING

1. *Sahoor*: To wake up at night and to eat and drink before the break of dawn. This is just like *Wudu* for prayer. While *wudu* is *Fard* for prayer, *Sahoor* is recommended for fasting.

2. Not to delay *Iftar* (the breaking of the fast), but to break one's fast right with sunset.

3. To make *Dua* when breaking fast.

4. To arrange *Iftar* for others.

5. To take a shower from *Janabat* before daybreak or from menses, or bleeding from childbirth, provided it stopped during the night so that the *Muslim* can start the fast in a pure and clean state. However, if for some reason it was not possible to do so, then it is still acceptable to start the fast.

6. To avoid vain talk and vain actions.

7. To be generous towards one's family, as well as the poor and needy.

8. To spend much time in recitation of the *Quran* and in the remembrance of *Allah*, and learning *Islam*.

9. To make *Itikaf* (retreat/seclusion) on the last ten days and nights at the *Masjid* for men and at home in the prayer place for women.

DISCOURAGED PRACTICES DURING FASTING

1. During *Nafl* fasting or optional fasting, not to fast as *Sawmul Wisal*, which means not to eat or drink for two consecutive days.

2. To gather saliva in the month intentionally and swallowing it. But swallowing saliva as a normal body reflex action is acceptable.

3. To taste something, even without swallowing, unless it is the utmost necessity.

4. To refrain from kissing one's spouse, to preclude the likelihood of enticing further passion.

ACCEPTABLE EXCUSES NOT TO FAST OR BREAK A FAST

1. TRAVELING:

Even though it is permissible not to fast while traveling, it is recommended that one continue the fast if possible.

2. SICKNESS:

When a pious *Muslim* physician recommends a patient not to fast for fear of aggravating their illness or condition.

3. PREGNANCY OR NURSING:

A pregnant woman or a woman nursing a baby must not endanger the health of her child or her own health by depriving her body of food.

4. OLD AGE:

When a person becomes so old that the body has become weak, and fasting would endanger the health or life of the person.

5. MEDICAL EMERGENCIES:

If a person has become dehydrated or weakened due to any reason that a *Muslim* physician feels that the person's life is in danger, then breaking a fast under such dire circumstances would be permissible.

6. THREAT OR FORCE:

In a circumstance where a person is threatened or forced to break his or her fast, it is permissible.

7. OTHER EMERGENCIES:

If a person must break his or her fast to rescue somebody from drowning or from a fire, then that is acceptable.

QADA IN FASTING

WHAT ARE THE THINGS THAT CAUSE BREAKING OF A FAST BUT REQUIRE *QADA* ONLY?

In general, there are only three kinds of circumstances that are applicable:

1. Eating, drinking or taking medicine all, with some acceptable excuse. For example, mistakenly swallowing water while making *Wudu*.

2. Eating or drinking something that is neither food nor medicine, whose nature does not require it to be eaten; for example, eating clay or inorganic materials.

3. Sexual discharge without sexual intercourse.

In all the above cases there is a *Qada* but no *Kaffarah* (expiation/atonement) due.

THINGS WHICH ENTAIL BOTH *QADA* AND *KAFFARAH*.

There are two primary actions that would necessitate this:

1. To consume food or drink or medicine without a valid excuse or need.

2. To satisfy oneself sexually while fasting.

In these two circumstances, a person is bound to do *Qada* as well as *Kaffarah*.

THINGS THAT DO NOT BREAK THE FAST

1. Eating or drinking by mistake or through thoughtlessness, not deliberately.

2. Using a toothbrush. But toothpaste may be avoided since some trace amount of the toothpaste can be swallowed.

3. An injection, either intramuscular or intravenous, does not break the fast. However, an enema does, since the intestine is connected to the stomach.

4. Vomiting does not break the fast. However, if the person vomits to the amount of a mouthful intentionally and swallows back a little bit, then according to *Imam Abu Hanifa* it does break the fast.

TARAWEEH

Taraweeh is a special prayer only offered in *Ramadan* after *Salat-e-Isha* and before *Salat-e-Witr* every night. *Taraweeh* is *Sunnah* and it consists of 20 *Rakat*. *Ibni Abbas* said that *Rasoolullah* used to offer 20 *Rakats* during *Taraweeh*. All the *Sahabah*, *Tabi'een*, *Mufasireen*, *Muhaddaseen*, all the four *Imams*, all the *Fuqaha*, and the entire *Muslim Ummah* for the last 14 centuries agree upon these 20 *Rakats*. As *farad Rakats* of all the five prayers every day along with the three *Witr Wajib* adds up to 20 *Rakats*, so in *Ramadan* an extra 20 *Rakats* are recommended as a *Sunnah*.

ITIKAF (SECLUSION)

Human beings, by nature, crave spiritual satisfaction. One of the ways to achieve this is through seclusion, where one completely disconnects oneself from the business of this world. And this is the reason that *Itikaf* is recommended for all men to stay at the *Masjid* from the 21st night of *Ramadan* until the night before *Eid* when its announcement is made. However, to stay until the *Eid* prayer is recommended. *Rasoolullah* (*Prophet Muhammad*) never missed *Itikaf* in *Ramadan*. Women can perform their *Itikaf* as well, at home in the place set aside for their prayer.

VIRTUES OF *RAMADAN*

There are many *Ahadith* regarding the virtues of *Ramadan*. Here we will select only one *Hadith* and provide some commentary.

Salman Al Farsi reported that *Rasoolullah* addressed us in the last day of the month of *Sha'ban* and he said

> *O People! There came upon you a great blessed month, a month wherein there is a night that is better than a thousand months. The fasting during this month is an obligation and the extra prayer at night is recommended. Anyone who comes close to Allah with good deeds in this month is as if he performed an obligatory duty during a time other than Ramadan. And he who fulfills an obligation during this month will be like he performed 70 obligatory duties in another month. It is a month of patience, and the reward of patience is Paradise. It is the month of sympathies (with the poor, sick and the needy) to share their sorrows. It is a month where the sustenance of a believer increases for whoever feeds a fasting person to break the fast for him. There shall be forgiveness of his*

sins and emancipation from the fire of hell, and for him his reward will not be diminished in the least." We said, *"O Messenger of Allah, not all of us can provide such things to a fasting person. The Messenger replied, "Allah grants this same reward to him who gives a single date or a drink of water or a sip of milk. This is a month, the first of which brings Allah's mercy, the middle brings his forgiveness, and the last part of which brings emancipation from the fire of hell. Whosoever lessens the burden of his slave or servant in this month, Allah will forgive him from the fire. And in this month four things you should increase to perform in great number. Two of which will please your Lord, while the other two shall be those without which you cannot make do. The former two are Kalima Tayeba and Istighfar, while the latter two are that you should ask Allah for entrance into Paradise and seek refuge in Him from the Fire of Jahannam. And whoever gives a person who fasted water to drink, Allah shall grant that giver to drink from My fountain, such a drink where after he shall never feel thirsty until he enters Jannah (Ibni Khuzaimah's Sahih).*

LAILAT UL QADR & EID UL FITR

Rasoolullah (Prophet Muhammad) said,

> *"Seek and search for the blessed night in the last ten nights from the month of Ramadan."*

And this is also another philosophy behind *Itikaf* as well. It is not essential for someone to recognize that night, but if he has performed *Ibadah* in that night without the knowledge that it is *Lailatul Qadr*, he will get the reward.

On the night before *Eid Allah* boasts about the fasting *Muslims* to the Angels.

> *"O My Angels! What is the reward of the worker who has done his job very well? They reply: O Lord, His reward should be given in full. To this Allah replies, "O My Angels, verily my servants have duly performed their duty there for they set forth to the Eid prayer ground, raising their voices in prayer to Me. I swear by My Honor, by My Grandeur, by My Grace and by My Exalted position that I shall surely forgive him."*

IMPORTANCE AND VIRTUES OF *RAMADAN*

The *Prophet (Muhammad) of Allah* said,

> *"Rajab (the month before Shaban) is the month of Allah, Shaban (the month before Ramadan) is my month, and Ramadan is the month of my Ummah (followers)."*

When the *Prophet Muhammad* sighted the crescent of *Rajab*, he made *Dua* (supplication) that

> *"Oh Allah bless us in the month of Rajab and Shaban and take us (alive) to the month of Ramadan."*

Ramadan is the month of *Qur'an* as the *Holy Qur'an* came from *Lau-I-Mahfuz* (the preserved tablet in a sacred place upon the seven heavens) to the nearest heaven in the month of *Ramadan*. Fasting has been an obligation in nearly every revealed religion, but in different ways and different months. Fasting in the month of *Ramadan* has been made mandatory for *Muslims*. The *Prophet* used to give due importance to this month and would fast therein.

Salman reports:

> *"On the last day of Shaban, the Prophet addressed us and said, 'Oh people, there has come to you now a great month, a most blessed month, in which there is a night which is greater than one thousand months (indicating that worship for one night is more rewarding than the worship of 1000 nights)."*

Ramadan is a month in which *Allah* has made fasting mandatory and He has made the *Qiyam* at night (*Taraweeh* prayers) as a *Sunnah*. Whosoever attempts to draw nearer to *Allah* by performing any virtuous deed in this month, for him shall be a great reward as if he had performed a *Fard* (mandatory practice) in any other month, and whosoever performs a *Fard*, for him will be a reward equivalent to seventy *Fard* in any other month. This is indeed the month of patience and stability, and the reward for true patience and stability is *Jannah* (paradise). It is the month of sympathy with one's fellow men; it is a month wherein a true believer's provision is increased.

To please your Lord, one should endeavor towards two things:

1) Recite the *Kalima Tayyib* (*La Ilaha Illallah*) in great quantity and,

2) Make as much *Istighfar* as you can (requesting *Allah* to forgive you and your sins).

Also, one must always request *Allah* for entry into paradise, and seek refuge with Him from the Hellfire.

In another *Hadith*, it is said that fasting is a shield (to protect one from torment).

Also, *Allah* said,

> *"Fasting is for Me alone (to please Me) and I give its reward", or, "Fasting is for Me alone, and I am its reward (meaning His pleasure)."*

The wisdom in fasting is to sanctify one's inner self, to strengthen his will power to break the fast (at sunset), for him there shall be forgiveness and emancipation from the fire of Hell, and the same reward applies to the one who was fed without his reward diminishing in the least.

Thereupon, the companions of the *Prophet* said,

> *"O Messenger of Allah, not all of us possesses the means to provide enough for a fasting person to break his fast."*

The Messenger of *Allah* replied,

> *"Allah grants this same reward to one who gives a fasting person a single date, or a drink of water, or a sip of milk to break the fast."*

The first part of this month is mercy (of *Allah*), the middle part is forgiveness, and the last part is emancipation from the hellfire. Whosoever lessens the burden of his servants (bondsmen) in this month; *Allah* will forgive him and free him from the fire. And whosoever gave a person who fasted water to drink, *Allah* shall grant him a drink from a fountain, which after drinking from; a person will never feel thirsty again until he enters Paradise.

PHILOSOPHY OF FASTING

The philosophy of fasting is as follows:

1. To sanctify one's inner self;

2. To strengthen his willpower;

3. To control his libido;

4. to gain patience and stability;

5. To find and feel the pain of hunger and thirst, and to sympathize with the poor as they feel the same pain all the time; and

6. To gain much more fear of *Allah* as this feeling is amplified in *Ramadan*.

There are also many rewards to fasting, among these being the Messenger said,

> *"Whosoever observed the fast combined with faith and the expectation of reward from Allah, all his past sins are forgiven."*

In another *Hadith* it is said,

> *"Whosoever did not give up lying and falsehood, Allah is in no need for him to give up food and water."*

SALAT UL TARAWEEH

The closest form of a *Muslim* to *Allah* is when he is in the form of *sajdah* (prayers).

The more *Sajdahs* he prays, the closer he will be to *Allah*.

The month of *Ramadan* is the month of the *Ummah*, as the *Prophet* of *Allah* said,

> *"A Nafl Ibadah in this month is equal to a Fard one."*

That is why the *Prophet* was eager to do *Ibadah* in this month.

Taraweeh at night in the month of *Ramadan* is a special *sunnah* prayer in this month.

Since the time of *Sahabah*, this prayer is the practice of *Ummah*.

Lately, some differences are arising as to how many *Rakat* is *Taraweeh*.

If someone misses *Taraweeh* for a valid reason, he will be pardoned by *Allah*; likewise, if someone prays a few *Rakat* and misses a few others, he will be pardoned as well. But one may not challenge this practice of 20 *Rakat*, as this is the constant practice of the *Ummah*, the *Sahabah, Tabi'een, Atbaut Tabi'een, Mujtahidin, Imams, Mufasireen, Muhadith-een, Fuqaha, Ulama,* and *Auliya*, and still that is the practice in *Masjidul Haram*, and *Masjidi Nabawi*.

This book is not a debate or challenge, but is written as an attempt to clarify and explain the actual position.

Salat Ut Taraweeh

The sources of *Islamic* Laws are:

The *Holy Quran*

The *Sunnah* of the *Prophet Muhammad*

The *Ijma*, consensus of the jurists

The *Qiyas*, analogical reasoning.

Then there are some other sources as well,

Aatharus Sahabah, the words and actions of *Sahabah*.

Urf, customs, usage, and convention.

Istihsan or preferences

The usual practice of *Madinites* or *Ta'aamuli Ahlul Medina*.

Istislah (welfare/public interest).

Istis'hab or linking

Ibadat or worship is the basic thing in Islam and there are various types:

A. *FARD* OR MANDATORY –

something that has been ordered in a certain text, i.e. the *Holy Quran* or a *Mutawatir Hadith* (narrated by a large number).

Such a text is called *Qat'I Uth – Thubut*, and when it expresses a sense and certain meanings, then that is called *Qat'I Ud Dalalah*.

So, one who does not practice the same is called a *Fasiq* (violator), and if someone denies the same, he becomes a disbeliever.

B. *WAJIB* OR COMPULSORY –

That which has been ordered in a text *Zanni Uth Thubut*, like *Khabari Wahid* (a specific type of *Hadith*). In practice this is as important as *Fard*, but if someone denies the same, he may not be declared a disbeliever, but one who has veered from the straight path.

For not practicing the *Fard* and *Wajib*, the punishment will be delivered on the *Day of Judgment*, unless *Allah* wills otherwise and forgives.

This distinction between *Fard* and *Wajib* is introduced by *Imam Abu Hanifa*, while to others these two terms are synonymous and mostly they use the *Wajib* for *Fard*. Very rarely they use *Fard* for the first category.

And even more rarely, they use *Wajib* for the second category. They use the term *Aakadus Sunan* for something that is lower than *Fard* and higher than regular *Sunnati Muakkadah*.

C. *SUNNATI MUAKKADAH* OR HIGHLY RECOMMENDED -

Sunnah is something the *Prophet Muhammad* used to do, but missed it once or twice in his lifetime. One who does not practice it may be blamed for on the *Day of Judgment*, and one who denied this concept loses his *Iman* and faith, but if someone denies a specific *Sunnah* it may be simply out of ignorance if he is not a scholar, or it may be his deduction if he is a jurist.

D. *MANDUB / MUSTAHAB* -

Mandub / Mustahab or recommended practice is something the *Prophet* used to do sporadically, because he liked it. So, one who does it, will be rewarded, but if he does not, then he will not be blamed.

E. *HARAM*, OR PROHIBITED -

This is a thing that has been clearly prohibited in a *Qat'I Ud Dalalah* text. So, it is the opposite of *Fard*. To abstain from such a thing or practice is *Fard*. If someone does it, then he is a sinner, and there will punishment on the *Day of Judgment*, unless he is forgiven by *Allah*. But if he did not believe it to be *Haram*, he loses his *Iman*. And if it is a violation of the due rights of a human, it must be pardoned by the said human, as *Allah* would not forgive a lack of pardon.

F. *MAKRUH* OR DISLIKED PRACTICE -

To *Imam Abu Hanifa* there are two types,

i. *MAKRUH - TAHREEMI*,

Makruh – Tahreemi, something that has been prohibited but in the text *Zanni Ud Dalalah,* clearly this is close to *Haram,* but lower. We can say this is like the opposite of *Wajib,* so one should abstain from that is all like *Haram,* but if someone does it, he may have swerved from the right path but may not be declared a disbeliever.

ii. *MAKRUH TANZEEHI*,

The *Sharia* asked not to do it as it is inappropriate, so to abstain from it will bring the abstainer a reward, but anyone who does it may not be punished for it.

According to others, *Makruh* is only *Tanzeehi*, while certain types of *Tahreemi* are either *haram* to them or *Tanzeehi* near them.

G. *MUBAH*, OR OPTIONAL -

As the *Sharia* neither ordered nor forbade it expressly or implicitly, it cannot be proven even by deduction.

Then, as we know if something is not crystal clear in *Quran* and Sunnah or is slightly ambiguous, then the general rule is that we consider the practice of *Sahabah*, (the companions of the *Prophet*), and if we see that their practice was unanimous, we may take it, and if they had different practices, in this regard the jurists have established rules to take one of these practices into consideration forever or take any one of them circumstantially.

For the same consideration they have established rules, called jurisprudence, as every law or legal system anywhere is known.

In *Ibadat*, the prayer is the ultimate worship and that is of four types: *Fard*, *Wajib*, *Sunnati Muakkadah*, and *mustahab*. Yes, there is the concept of *Haram* and *Makruh* prayers also, when it is prohibited in times or places or fell short of its requirements.

Salat Ut Taraweeh is a prayer in the month of *Ramadan* that comes after *Isha* prayer. It is *Sunnah Muakkadah*, as the *Prophet* used to do it and exhorted others to do so as well. As *Abu Hurairah* narrated that the *Prophet Muhammad* said,

> *"Whosoever did Qiyam [prayed at night] during Ramadan with Iman and Ihtisab, whatever sin he has done before is forgiven (Muslim, Abu Dawud)."*

Iman is the base for each good deed to be accepted as there is no value and weight of even the good deed or a disbeliever. *Ihtisab* means a belief virtue for its own reward, or it means self-accountability, as that is the philosophy of fasting.

Also, the *Prophet Muhammad* said,

> *"This is a month which Allah has made its fasting mandatory and its Qiyam Ul Lail, [prayer at night] a Tatawwu [recommendation]."*

Bayhaqi and *Ibni Khuzaimah* narrated this from *Salman Farsi*.

Also, *Imam Nisa'i* narrated a *Hadith* that the *Prophet Muhammad* said,

> *"Verily Allah has made the fasting in Ramadan mandatory and I have made its Qiyam, a Sunnah."*

Based on these *Ahadith*, this prayer at night during *Ramadan* is *Sunnah*.

HOW *PROPHET MUHAMMAD* PERFORMED *QIYAM*

HOW DID *PROPHET MUHAMMAD* PERFORM THIS *QIYAM*?

Abu Hurairah said,

> *The Messenger of Allah used to make a case for Qiyam in Ramadan without ordering it strongly. The Prophet of Allah passed away and this was the case, then was the case in the time of Abu Bakr, and in the beginning of the time of Umar.*

It means that the *Prophet Muhammad* used to do it individually and exhort others to do so, and the practice was the same in the time of *Abu Bakr* and *Umar*.

So, this was a *Sunnah* but on individual basis.

But the Messenger of *Allah* also did the same in *Jama'at*, (congregation), as *Imam Bukhari* narrates this from *Aaisha*.

> *The Messenger of Allah came out one night and prayed in the "Masjid", and [some] men prayed with his prayer*

[behind him], then people spoke about that the next day. More people gathered, then he [the Prophet] prayed and they prayed with him. Then people spoke about it the next morning, so lots of people gathered together for the third night. The Messenger of Allah came out and prayed, and the people prayed with his prayer. Then when it was the fourth night, the "Masjid" became empty of people till he [the Prophet] came out for morning prayer. When he prayed the Fajr, [morning prayer], he faced the people, recited Tashah'hud and said, "and after [this] I had no concern of yours being [in Masjid and waiting the whole night], but I was concerned that if I will lead you in Qiyam tonight as well, it will be made mandatory for you people, and you could not do it. So, after the Prophet passed away, this was the case, praying it individually.

Abu Zar related,

We fasted with the Messenger of Allah in Ramadan, he did not lead us [in night prayer] until there remained 7 days of the month. So, then he led us till a third of the night was gone, then he did not lead us on the sixth night, [24th of Ramadan]. then he led us on the fifth night, [25th of Ramadan] until half of the night was gone, so I said, O the Messenger of Allah, would increase for us the Nafl prayer for the remaining part of this night as well? He said, whosoever stood with Iman [for prayer] till he finished, Allah will put on record for him as having prayed all night. Then he did not lead us (on 26th of Ramadan) till there remained only three [nights] in the month, so he *led us on the third [27th of Ramadan], (and he said 3rd as mostly the month is of 29 day) and Ibni Masud said in a Hadith that we fasted with the Prophet only twice in 30 days. So, the remaining were 29 days only, and he gathered his family and wives [praying] till we feared we may miss the Falah. I said, (Jubair Ibni Nujaym, the narrator from Abu Zar) what is Falah? He said, Sahur [eating at night after fasting] (Abu Dawud, Nisa'i, Tirmizi).*

Imam Nisa'i narrates from *Numan Ibni Bashir* that he said while on the pulpit in *Homs* (a city in *Sham/Syria*).

We stood up (to pray) in the month of Ramadan on the 23rd night up to 1/3rd of the night was gone, then we stood up with him on the 25th up to half of the night was gone, then we stood up with him on the 27th till we thought we cannot catch "Falah", and they used to call it "Sahur."

Imam Bukhari, *Imam Muslim*, *Abu Dawud*, and *Nisa'i* narrated from *Zaid Ibni Thabit* the prayer of the *Prophet* with people one night only, and the like of that *Imam Muslim* narrate from *Anas*.

Now it is proven that the *Prophet* himself was eager to do more and more *Ibadat*, specially the *Qiyam*, and *salat*, but how many *Rakat* of *Taraweeh* did he perform?

Imam Haithami related this, and the same is related by *Tabrani* and *Abu Yala* from *Jabir*, that the *Prophet* prayed 8 *Rakat* and *Witr*. But in the narration chain of this narration there is *Isa Ibni Jariyah*, and he is *Mutafarrid* in this narration.

Imam Yahya Ibni Ma'een, the critic, said, that he is not very reliable and he has *Manakir* (plural of *Munkar*, a type of *Hadith Daeef*).

Imam Abu Dawud said, *Munkar Ul Hadith*, and said, *Matruk*, (another type of *Zaeef* (weak) narrator). *Imam Saaji* and *Imam Aqeeli* both mentioned *Isa Ibni Jariyah* as a weak narrator.

Ibni Adi said,

> "His hadith is not secured."

Also, *Ibni Kathir* said, in chain there is another narrator, *Yaqub Ibni Abdullah Al Haithami*, he is from the *Shia* sect, and this is *Tafarrud*, (a type of narrator where one narrates something other than what an authentic narrator narrated), which is not accepted.

Also, it could be said that he mentioned only one night, so it is possible that the *Prophet* already had prayed more, as that is mentioned in the narration of *Anas* which *Al Haithami* related in *Majma Az Zawa'id* with reference to *Imam Tabrani*, and said its narrators are the narrators of *Sahih*, (accepted *hadith* or book).

Imam Bayhaqi narrated from *Ibni Abbas*,

> "That the Messenger of Allah prayed in the month of Ramadan without Jama'at *(congregation) 20 Rakat and Witr."*

Also, *Ibni Abi Shaibah* narrated that the same in *Musanaf Volume 2*.

But there in this *Hadith Ibrahim Ibni Uthman (Abu Shaibah)*, he is *Zaeef*, (weak).

But we say that the *Ummat* since the time of *Umar* adopted this practice continuously, never broken by any generation. So, this practice became *Mutawatir*, and this is called *Mutawatir Amalan*, or *Talaqqi Bil – Qabul*. Also, this practice from generation to generation is called *Ta'aamul*, and the *Ummah* has taken *Ta'aamul* as a source of Sharia, and especially that of the first three best generations.

This *Ta'aamul* was ongoing, but in the 14th century, some people brought the idea of 8 *Rakat* based upon a misinterpretation of a *Hadith*, which we will talk about it later.

The *Sanad* (chain) of this *Hadith* of *Ibni Abbas* is *Yazeed Ibni Harun*, from *Ibrahim Ibni Uthman*, from *Hikm*, from *Maqsum*, from *Abbas*.

Imam Bukhari narrated that *Abu Salamah Ibni Abdur Rahman* asked *Aisha* about the prayer of the *Prophet* in *Ramadan*, so she said,

> *That he used not to exceed in Ramadan or in any other (month) 11 Rakat, praying four. So, ask not of its beauty and time then praying four, so ask not of its beauty and time then praying three (Rakat). So, I said, "O the Messenger of Allah! Do you sleep before Witr? He said, "O Aisha, my eyes are sleeping but my heart does not."*

Imam Bukhari narrated this *Hadith* once in chapter *Salat Ut Taraweeh*, the same one he narrated in chapter *Qiyam* of the *Prophet Muhammad* at night in *Ramadan* and other. And the third place he narrated it is in the chapter that begins,

"*The eyes of the Prophet were sleeping, not his heart.*"

This one is the only *Riwayat*. To those who say *Taraweeh* is 8 *Rakat*, we say that this plea needs a few more questions asked before it can be answered.

Is the same prayer worth 8 *Rakat* is the *Tahajjud* at times other than *Ramadan*, and it is the *Taraweeh* in *Ramadan*? If the answer is affirmative, we then ask whether the *Prophet* used not to pray any *Tahajjud* in *Ramadan*, but only *Taraweeh*, while he used to be more eager for *Ibadat* in *Ramadan*?

The same prayer as *Tahajjud* was a *Nafl* prayer in other than *Ramadan*, and it is *Sunnah* in *Ramadan*

Furthermore, we say that this *Hadith* says, The *Prophet* used not to exceed eleven *Rakat* in *Ramadan* and other months, but there is another *Hadith* by *Imam Abu Dawud* from *Abdullah Ibni Abi Qais*, wherein I asked *Aaisha*, how many *Rakat* did the *Prophet* to do for *Witr*.

She said, He used to do it four and three, six and three, eight and three, and ten and three.

So, the three was *Witr*, and before that it was *Nafl*, which means that he was praying 10 *Rakat Qiyam* as well. Also, in a narration of *Ibni Abbas* it is said that he did twelve and three.

Now it is clear that the *Hadith* of *Aaisha* is regarding *Tahajjud*, and the number of *Rakat* is different in her narration. So, this is not an *Idtiraab* in *Hadith*, but it means that the *Prophet* used to pray different number of *Rakat* at *Tahajjud*.

The *Hadith* of *Aisha* being in *Tahajjud* is very much clear as the majority of *Muhaditheen* narrated this *Hadith*, but none of them has mentioned it in the chapter of *Taraweeh*.

None of them has said that *Taraweeh* and *Tahajjud* both are one and the same, but two different types of prayer, as they wrote two chapters in their books. One the chapter of *Tahajjud* or *Qiyam Ul Lail*, and the other one regarding *Taraweeh* or *Qiyam Ul Lail* in *Ramadan*.

All the *Fuqaha* and compilers of books in *Fiqh* of all four schools have written two different chapters for Taraweeh and *Tahajjud*. So, from *Muhaditheen* who wrote two different chapters there are a few big names:

Imam Muslim, Imam Malik, Abu Dawud, Tirmizi, Nisa'i, Abdur Razaq, Abu Awanah, Khuzaimah, Addarimi Ibni Hajar Al-Khatib, and all of them narrated this *Hadith* from *Malik Ibni Anas*. But *Malik* used to pray 36 *Rakat Taraweeh* as it was the *Ta'aamul* of the people of *Medina* (*Medina*), as the people of *Medina* are those who observed the *Prophet*. Then the first three successors of the *Prophet* and the fourth one for some time until he took the capital to *Kufa*.

Then the people of *Medina* once said to their scholars, maybe in the time of *Tabi'een*, that people in *Makkah* (*Mecca*) pray 20 *Rakats* having four times *Tarweeha* after every four *Rakat*, and in that *Tarweeha*, they make *Tawaf* around the *Kabah*. We do not have that opportunity, so the scholars said, lets pray another 4 *Rakat* in that *Tarweeha*. In such a way that they were praying sixteen extra *Rakat*. Later, we will mention the reason for 36 *Rakat* as well.

Then those *Muhaditheen* who related this *Hadith* of *Aisha* in chapter of *Qiyami Ramadan*, they also wrote separate chapters for *Taraweeh*, and *Tahajjud*, which means to pray *Tahajjud* and *Taraweeh* both in *Ramadan*.

Khatib Baghdadi wrote in his *Tareekh* (history book), that *Imam Bukhari* used to pray both as well.

And if it was the case that the *Prophet* used to pray 8 *Rakat Taraweeh* in *Ramadan*, then when *Umar* gathered the *Sahabah* over 20 *Rakat*, then why *Aisha* did not take a plea while she was the *Faqeehatul Ummah*, (jurist), and the *Sahabah*, including *Umar*, used to consult her?

Nobody made any objection, neither in the time of *Umar* nor in the time of *Uthman* and *Ali*, referring to this *Hadith*. All these *Khulafa* (successors) were very kind, good listeners of the truth, especially when it came to the words of the *Prophet*.

Such was the case in the time of *Tabi'een*, as we will mention, and nobody objected then either.

Furthermore, we say that the *Hadith* of *Ibni Abbas*, which we mentioned already has *Ibrahim Ibni Uthman* in it and he is *Zaeef*, but the *Ummah* took it into consideration, so that weakness is gone, which is a well-known rule in *Usul Ul Hadith*.

Also regarding the number and any type of measurement and anything which could not be known through sense and intellect when a companion says it or practices it even without attributing the same to the *Prophet*, that is considered *Marfu* (something related from the *Prophet*).

When there is an issue that is slightly ambiguous, then for clarification this is also a well-known rule, to go to the practice of the companions, especially regarding numbers and measurement.

As for the saying of *Umar* is concerned, when he gathered over 20 *Rakat* behind *Ubai Ibni Ka'b* and said,

> *"What a good Bid'at (innovation) this is."*

He was not referring to the number of *Rakat*, for if someone started praying 100 *Rakat* at night in *Ramadan* or any other month, no one could say this is *Bid'at*. So, he meant to have it in *Jama'at* for the whole month as the *Prophet* did the same for 3 nights only, as we said before, and now there was no fear of it becoming mandatory.

TARAWEEH IN THE TIME OF *KHULAFAH-I-RASHIDIN*

Imam Bukhari narrated from *Abdur Rahman Ibni Abdul Qais* that I came with *Umar Ibnul Khattab* one night in *Ramadan* to the *Masjid* and the people were scattered in groups: one was praying by himself, another one was joined in his prayer by a group, so *Umar* said,

> *"I think if I can gather these people behind one Qari (imam), it will be good. Then he planned and gathered them behind Ubai Ibni Ka'b. I came with him another night and the people were praying behind their Qari, so Umar said what a good Bid'at (innovation) this is, and that [prayer] which from the people are sleeping is better than that one they pray, [the one in the first part of the night]."*

This practice started in year 14th after *Hijra*, i.e. the 2nd year of the rule of *Umar*.

This is there in *Tareekul Khulafa* of *Sayuti* and *Tareekh* of *Ibnul Atheer*.

BUT, HOW MANY *RAKAT* DID THEY PRAY?

Sa'ib Ibni Yazeed relates it, and three of his students narrated the same from him: *Harith Ibni Abdur Rahman Ibni Abi Ziyad, Yazeed Ibni Abi Khusaifa,* and *Muhammad Ibni Yusuf.*

Then the narration of *Haarith* is narrated by *Imam Badrud Din Al Aini* in *Umdatul Qari, Volume 11,* that *Sa'ib Ibni Yazeed* said,

> "*Qiyam (Taraweeh) in the time of Umar was 23 Rakat.*"

Then *Ibni Abdul Barr* said that 3 *Rakat* of it was *Witr*.

The *Riwayat* of *Yazeed Ibni Abi Khusaifa* is narrated by his three students: *Ibni Abi Zi'b, Muhammad Ibni Jafar,* and *Imam Malik Ibni Anas.*

The *Riwayat* of *Ibni Abi Zi'b* relates that *Sa'ib Ibni Yazeed* said,

> *They [Sahabah] used to do Qiyam in the time of Umar, in the month of Ramadan by 20 Rakat (with Jama'at), and they used to recite hundreds of Ayat (in each Rakat), and they used to lean on their walking sticks in the time of Uthman due to length of the Qiyam.*

This is narrated by *Bayhaqi* and as we said, it is *Sanad* according to *Imam Nawai, Imam Iraqi,* and *Imam Sayuti* is *Sahih* (*Aatharus Sunan, Volume 2,* and *Tuhfatul Ahwazi, Volume 2*).

The *Riwayat* of *Muhammad Ibni Jafar* from *Yazeed Ibni Khusaifa* is also related by *Bayhaqi* in his book *Marifatus - Sunani Wal Aathar* wherein *Sa'ib Ibni Yazeed* said,

> "We used to do Qiyam (with Jama'at) in the time of Umar by 20 Rakat and Witr."

Its *Sanad* is also *Sahih* according to *Nawawi*, as is in *Al Khulasah Alat-Tahzeeb*, *Sabuki* in *Sharhul Munhaj*. Also, *Allama Ali Al Qazi*, in his explanation of *Mu'atta* as mentioned in *Aatharus Sunan, Volume 2*, and *Tuhfatul Ahwazi, Volume 2*.

The *Riwayah* of *Malik Ibni Anas* from *Sa'ib Ibni Yazeed* also mentions 20 *Rakat* as *Hafiz Ibni Hajar* related the same in *Fathul Bari, Volume 4*, and *Allama Shaukani* in *Nailul Autar Volume 3*.

This *Sanad* is there in the book of *Imam Bukhari*, so *Sanad* is *Sahih*, but this *Riwayah* is not there in *Mu'atta*, as *Imam Malik* compiled his book from the thousands of *Ahadith* he had, but he did not include all of them.

Yes, the 3rd student of *Sa'ib Ibni Yazeed*, namely *Muhammad Ibni Yusuf's* students, differed from each other, so in the *Riwayah* of *Malik* it is said that *Umar* ordered *Ubai Ibni Ka'b* and *Tameem Addari* to pray 11 *Rakat* as it is in *Mu'atta*.

Ibni Ishaq relates that it is 13 *Rakat*, as it is in *Musannaf* of *Abdur Razaq, Volume 4*.

In the *Riwayat* of *Dawud Ibni Qais*, there are 21 *Rakat* as it is also in *Mu'atta*.

Now the *Riwayat* of *Muhammad Ibni Yusuf* is *Mudtarab* (confused, disturbed, and a type of *Zaeef*), so it may not be taken into consideration as this is the rule, or may be explained in the light of other *Sahih Ahadith* to have a patch up there in.

That is why *Bayhaqi* said that they did *Qiyam* by eleven *Rakat*, and later by 20 and *Witr* (*As Sunanal Kubra Volume 2*).

Now it is clear that in the time of *Umar*, the established practice was 20 *Rakat* as *Imam Malik*, the very narrator from *Muhammad Ibni Yusuf*, used to pray 36 *Rakat* or 20 *Rakat* at least.

Ibni Ishaq, the other student also said regarding 20 *Rakat's Riwayat*.

And this is the much more established *Riwayat* I heard in this regard.

Furthermore, there is no any other support for the *Riwayat* of 11 *Rakat* by *Sa'ib*, while there are many supportive narrations for his *Riwayat* of 20 *Rakat*.

Yazeed Ibni Roman said that people used to do *Qiyam* by 23 *Rakat* in the time of *Umar* (*Mu'atta*).

The *Sanad* is okay, but *hadith* is *Mursal*, as *Yazeed* was not there in this time of *Umar*, and *Mursal* is okay according to *Jumhur* if its *Sanad* is okay, except *Imam Shafi* said,

> "*Mursal* is okay if it has been supported by other *Mursal*, or *Musnad*, and this hadith has much support, while the *Mursal* in *Mu'atta* is okay according to scholars."

Muhammad Ibni Ka'b Al Qurazi also narrates 20 *Rakat Taraweeh*, and 3 *Witr* in the time of *Umar* (*Qiyam Ul Lail*).

Yahya Ibni Saeed Al Ansari said that *Umar* ordered one man to lead them for 20 *Rakat* (*Musannaf Ibni Abi Shaibah, Volume 2*).

Abdul Aziz Ibni Rafi said, *Ubai Ibni Ka'b* used to lead people in *Ramadan* at *Medina* by 20 *Rakat Taraweeh*, and 3 *Witr*.

Ubai Ibni Ka'b said that *Umar* ordered him to pray at night in *Ramadan* and said people fast at daytime, and do *Qiyam* at night, but cannot recite in a good way, so if you will recite (and lead). I said this (*Jama'at* in *Qiyam*) is a thing not in past. He said I know but this is good so he (*Ubai*) led them in 20 *Rakat* (*Kanzul Ummal, Volume 8*).

If this last *Hadith* is *Zaeef*, it is still valid for support.

Abu Dawud narrated from *Hasan* that *Umar* gathered people behind *Ubai Ibni Ka'b* and used to lead them in 20 *Rakat*.

In *Al Mudawwanatul Kubra* it is said that *Umar* and *Uthman* used to do *Taraweeh* in *Ramadan* with people.

Bayhaqi narrated from *Abu Abdur Rahman As Sullami* that *Ali* called the *Qaris*, he then ordered one of them to lead people in 20 *Rakat*, and *Ali* used to lead them in *Witr* (*Bayhaqi, Volume 2*).

The same thing is narrated from *Abul Hasana* that *Ali* did it as this is in *Musannaf* of *Ibni Abi Shaibah, Volume 2*.

So, this is the practice of three *Khulafa*.

Hafiz Ibni Taymiyyah said,

> "It has been proven that Ubai used to lead people in 20 Rakat, and 3 Witr, therefore the scholars (jurists) have

said that this is sunnah as he led Muhajireen and Ansar, and not a single one objected to him (Al Fatwa Volume 1)."

Also, *Hafiz Ibni Taymiyyah* related this *Hadith* of *As Sullami* in *Minhajus Sunnah*, and said it means that *Ali* kept the practice of *Jama'at* established in the time of *Umar*. Also, *Zahabi* said in *Al Muntaqa* that the saying of *Ibni Taymiyyah* means that this practice was going on in the time of *Ali*.

The same practice of *Ali* is narrated by *Imam Zaid* in his *Musnad* from *Zaid Ibni Ali*, from his father, and he narrates from his grandfather.

Bayhaqi related from *Abul Hasana* that *Ali* commanded a man to lead people in prayer 20 *Rakat* with 5 *Tarweeha*.

Then *Bayhaqi* said, in this *Hadith* there is *Abu Saeed Al Baqqal*, and he is *Zaeef*, but the same practice of 20 is narrated by *Amr Ibnul Qais* from *Abul Hasana* as we mentioned in number 9, that one is its *Mutabi* (support).

Then *Tarweeha* used to take place after every 4 *Rakat*, which means they used to do the same after 20 *Rakat*, and before *Witr* as well.

Zaid Ibni Ali in his afore said *Riwayat* also mentioned *Tarweeha* after every 4 *Rakat*.

The practice of *Sahabah* and *Tabi'een*

Zaid Ibni Wahab said,

"Ibni Masud used to lead us in the Month of Ramadan."

Imam Aamash said he used to pray 20 *Rakat* (*Qiyam Ul Lail* by *Ibnus Sani*).

Now this is the practice of *Sahabah* whom the *Prophet* said,

> *So, you may be committed to my* sunnah, *and the* sunnah *of righteous guided successors. All* Sahabah *were his successors in Deen (Abu Dawud, Tirmizi).*

TABI'EEN

FROM AMONGST *TABI'EEN* A FEW ARE:

Abul Khusaib said that *Suwaid Ibni Ghafalah* used to lead us in *Ramadan* 20 *Rakat* with 5 *Tarweehat*.

Bayhaqi in *As Sunan Ul Kubra*, and *Neemawi* said its chain is *Hasan*.

This *Suwaid* is not *Tabi'ee* only, but he is *Mukhdram*. He was in the time of the *Prophet* came to *Medina* the day the *Prophet* passed away. Then he stayed in *Kufa* in the company of *Ibni Masud*, and later *Ali*, and passed away in year 80 after *Hijra* at the age of 130.

> *Haarith* used to lead people in Ramadan for 20 Taraweeh and three Witr, and used to do Qunut before Ruku (Ibni Abi Shaibah, Volume 2, Qiyam Ul Lail).

> *Shittir Ibni Shakal* used to lead people in 20 Rakat Taraweeh, and three Witr (As Sunan Al Kubra, Volume 2, Qiyam Ul Lail).

Shittir was a follower of *Ali*.

Abul Bukhtari a

> *"Tabi'ee used to pray with five Tarweehat, (meaning 20 Rakat), and three Witr (Ibni Abi Shaibah, Volume 2)."*

Ata, said,

> *"I found people praying 23 Rakat with Witr (Musannaf, Volume 2)."*

Nafi Ibni Umar said that Ibni Abi Mulaika used to lead them during Ramadan in 20 Rakat (Ibni Abi Shaiba, Volume 2, Aatharus-Sunan, Volume 2).

Saeed Ibni Ubaid says that Ali Ibni Rabi'a used to lead them in Ramadan with five Tarweehat, and do Witr three Rakat (Ibni Abi Shaibah).

Imam Abu Hanifa relates from Hammad, and he from Ibrahim that people used to pray 5 Tarweehat in Ramadan, 20 Rakat, and do Witr 3 Rakat (Bayhaqi, Volume 2).

Abdur Rahman Ibni Abi Bakrah, the student of Ali used to lead people with 5 Tarweehat, 20 Rakat (Qiyam Ul Lail).

Saeed Ibnul Hasan, a famous student of Ali, used to lead people in 20 Rakat with 5 Tarweehat (Qiyam Ul Lail).

Imran Al Aabidi used to lead people in 20 Rakat (Qiyam Ul Lail).

He was also a disciple of *Ali*. These three students of *Ali* used to do an extra *Tarweeha* in the last 10 days.

The word *Tarweehat* is the plural of *Tarweeha*. This plural is a broken plural, which means at least more than three *Tarweeha*. This is *Tafeel* of *Rauh* which means rest and relaxation. So, after every four *Rakat* they used to take a rest, and be relaxed after standing for a long time, and *Ibadat* should be performed in a relaxed way.

This word is used by *Aisha* as she said,

> "So he (the Prophet) used to pray 4 Rakat, then he used to take a rest and get relaxed, and he did it for a long time."

We already related the *Riwayat* where there in the word *Tarweehat* is used by the students of *Sahabah*. Then the jurists, *Muhaditheen*, and *Fuqaha* (scholars in *Fiqh*), used this term frequently as they named the chapter, the chapter of *Taraweeh*.

This term *Salat Ut Taraweeh*, is like that of *Salat Uz Zuhr*, attributed to its day or *Salat Ul Istisqaa*, attributed to its purpose (asking for rainfall), or *Salat Ul Kusuf*, attributed to its cause and reason (the sun of moon eclipse). This one is attributed to *Tarweehat* as it is noticed because it happens after every four *Rakat*.

THE PRACTICE OF JURISTS

These twenty *Rakat* is the practice of all *Fuqaha* and jurists, and of the four founders of schools of Jurisprudence: *Abu Hanifa, Malik, Shafi,* and *Ahmad*.

Imam Tirmizi said,

> "The people of knowledge differed in Qiyami Ramadan; some of them are of the view to pray 41 Rakat with Witr, which was the practice of the inhabitants of Medina, while the majority of people of knowledge believe it is what is related from Ali, Umar, and other Sahabah of the Prophet. This is what Sufyan, Abdullah Ibnul Mubarak, Shafi said. Imam Shafi also said the same way (practice), "I found at our city Makkah that they pray 20 Rakat."

So, the 20 *Rakat* is *Ijma*, while the aforementioned 41 *Rakat* means two *Sunnah* of *Isha*, 20 *Rakat Taraweeh*, and 16 *Rakat Nafl* in four *Tarweehat*, in between, and 3 *Witr*.

Also, the people of *Medina* added another *Tarweeha* of 4 *Rakat* at the time of *Harrah*.

Allama Zurqan related from *Abul Waleed Sulaiman Ibni Khalaf Al Baji* that they were commanded to perform a long recitation in the beginning, but when it became hard for them, then they were ordered to reduce the recitation in each *Rakat*, and to add the *Rakat*, so they started 23 *Rakat*.

> *Then this was the practice till the time of Harrah, so again they reduced the recitation and added Rakat, and made it 36 Rakat, plus 3 Witr (Az Zurqani, Volume 1).*

Also, he related the like of that from *Abu Marwan Abdul Malik Ibni Habib Al Qurtubi Al Maliki*, and *hafiz Ibni Abdul Barr*.

Hafiz Ibni Qudamah Al Madisi Al Hambali said,

> *"For us is, that Umar when he gathers people behind Ubai Ibni Ka'b, he used to pray for them 20 Rakat, and after relating a few Riwayat,"*

and, the *Athar* of *Ali*, he said,

> *"And this is like an ijma;"*

while regarding the *Ta'aamul* of the people, of *Medina* he said,

> *"Then if it is proven that all people in Medina did practice the same, then what Umar did and Sahabah accepted that unanimously in his time is prior to be followed, while some scholars said that the people of Medina tried to be equal to the people of Makkah as the people of Makkah used to make seven rounds of tawaf around the Kabah in each Tarweeha. So, the people of Medina put 4 Rakat*

there, but what the companions of the Prophet used to do is the utmost priority (Al Mughni, Volume 1)."

Imam Nawawi is a *Shafiti*; he wrote in *Al Majmu, Volume 4*, that

"our Ulama took a plea based on what Bayhaqi and others related with authentic chain from Sa'ib Ibni Yazeed that they used to pray 20 Rakat in the time of Umar in Ramadan."

After this he quoted the *Riwayat* of *Yazeed Ibni Roman*, the emendation between two narrations by *Bayhaqi* (mentioned before), the *Athar* of *Ali*, and he mentioned the reason for the practice of the people of *Medina*, like that of *Ibni Qudamah*.

Qustulani Ash Safi said that

Bayhaqi made an emendation between Riwayat that they used to pray 11 Rakat, and later on they used to pray 20 Rakat (Taraweeh), three Rakat Witr. And they considered the practice in the time of Umar as ijma (Irshad us Sari Alal Bukhari, Volume 3).

Allama Al Bahuti Al Hambali writes:

That (Taraweeh) is twenty Rakat as Malik narrated from Yazeed Ibni Roman that people in the time of Umar used to pray 23 Rakat in Ramadan, and this is Mashhur, so it was an Ijma (Kash'Shaful Qina, Volume 1).

THE PRACTICE OF THE FOUR *IMAMS*

As a preface we say that no one is a *Shari* but *Allah*, who gives laws and rules, while the Messenger of *Allah* is considered a *Shari* as what he orders, he does the same based on *Wahi*, but he is *Sharih* also, who explains the laws and rules.

Other than the *Prophet* the authentic scholars and jurists are the *Shariheen* only. Four of them, namely *Abu Hanifa, Malik, Shafi,* and *Ahmad,* were accepted by *Allah,* so the *Ummah* follows their deductions, explanations, interpretations, and applications.

All of them said that *Taraweeh*, in the light of *sunnah* is 20 *Rakat*. Yes, *Imam Malik* himself practiced 36 *Rakat*, as it was the *Ta'aamul* of the people of *Medina*.

Allama Ali Al Qari said

> *Sahabah agreed upon 20 Rakat unanimously (Mirqatul Mafateeh, Volume 3).*

Then this is *Sunnah*, as *Sahabah* did not innovate anything on their own.

Also, there are logical reasons for this number, as *Salman* relates that the *Prophet* said,

> *"whosoever did one mandatory practice there in this month, he is as if he has done 70 mandatory practices in any other month than Ramadan, and whosoever did a recommended practice therein, he is as if he has done a mandatory practice in any other month than Ramadan."*

And as we know that mandatory prayers are 17 *Rakat*, as 2 plus 4 plus 4 plus 3 plus 4, and 3 *Rakat Witr* which is practically like that of *Fard*, but that is *Wajib*, so all together the number is 20. Now, this number is doubled in *Ramadan* by 20 *Rakat Taraweeh* as *Ibni Nujaym* related this from *Allama Halbi*, the *Hanafi* jurist. While *Allama Bahuti*, the *Hambali* jurist, said that *Sunnati Mu'akkad* throughout the whole day is 10 *Rakat*, which is agreed upon by all four schools, to *Abu Hanifa* this number is 12 *Rakat*, but at least he agreed upon 10 *Rakat* with others, so that number is doubled in *Ramadan*.

Imam Wali Ullah said that the *Prophet* did 11 *Rakat Qiyam* at night throughout the whole year, so in *Ramadan* this number is doubled as well.

SALAT UL WITR

As we know that *Allah* sent His messengers to guide humanity to the right path and to teach them how to get more and more closer to *Allah* through *Ibadat* (worship).

Ibadat prayer is the first ever and most important worship. *Sahabah* used to look at the *Prophet* of *Allah*, what he does. They started emulating him and practicing the same without putting it into categories like *Fard*, *Sunnah*, etc. or even to think of it that he did so as a habit and not as *Ibadah*, and that is why *Allah* said:

> "*Allah is pleased with them and they are pleased with Allah (At-Taubah).*"

May *Allah* have his Mercy on the jurists of *Ummah* that they not only explained the *Sharia*, but based on the Rules of Jurisprudence, they fixed the categories of different types of *Ibadat*, saying this one is *Fard*, that one is *Wajib*, that one is *Sunnah*, etc. So, let's see as a preface how they classified it.

This classification is based upon Commandments and Prohibitions: *Fard* or mandatory practice is that which is mentioned in a *Qat'I* (certain) text, having no doubt, confusion or complication in its explanation or application. One who does not practice the same is considered *Fasiq* (violator) while one who denied it is considered *Kafir* (disbeliever).

Wajib, or compulsory practice, is that one which is mentioned there in a *Zanni* (uncertain / *Khabari Wahid*) text. Practice-wise this is the same as *Fard*. So, one who does not do the same is *Fasiq* (violator), while faith-wise, that is lower than *Fard*. So, one who denied it is not considered *Kafir* (disbeliever). So, one who does not practice the *Fard* or *Wajib* would be punished.

Sunnah Al Muakkadah or highly recommended practice is that one which the *Prophet* used to do constantly, but he missed it once or twice in his lifetime.

Mustahab, or liked and recommended practice, is that which the *Prophet* did on an on-and-off basis, but he called towards it expressly or implicitly.

Haram, or forbidden, is that practice which is prohibited in a *Qat'I* (certain) text having no confusion in its explanation or application. One who will not abstain from it is considered a *Fasiq* (violator) and the one who did not believe it as *"forbidden"* is considered *Kafir* (disbeliever).

Makruh Tahreemi, or that practice which is disliked and is close to *haram*. This is that one which is forbidden in a *Zanni* (uncertain) text. It is like *Haram* practice-wise. So, its doer is considered a *Fasiq*. But if he denied it, he is not considered a *Kafir*.

Makruh Tanzeehi, or disliked practice is one whose abstinence is recommended, so it should be avoided.

Mubah, or optional, the doing of which or abstinence from it is not known in *Sharia* neither expressly nor implicitly and not even through deduction, so that is up to the individual whether it is permissible.

All these details and classification is according to *Hanafites*, while *Jumhur* (those other than *Hanafites*) use the terms *Fard* and *Wajib* interchangeably, but even they use the word *Fard* for this purpose very rarely. Mostly they use the term *Wajib*. But for something which is higher in grade than *Sunnah Al Muakkadah* according to them, then sometimes they use the term *Aakadus Sunan* (extremely and highly recommended practice) and this term is almost close to the concept of *Wajib* according to *Hanafites*.

Likewise, the *Jumhur* did not use the term *Makruh Tahreemi*; rather they used the term *Makruh* and they meant the *Tanzeehi* one.

Also, as we know that sources of *Sharia* are:

The Book of *Allah*;

The *Sunnah* of the *Prophet*;

The *Ijma* (consensus of jurists); and

The *Qiyas* (analogical reasoning).

They added to it the following:

The *Aatharus Sahaba* (sayings and practices of *Sahabah*);

The *Sharia* of those before use;

The Preferences;

The public interest;

The *Urf* (custom or convention)

The *Istidlal* (finding evidence);

The *Istiqra* (research); and

The *Isti'habul Hal* (linking to the past).

Then if something has some ambiguity as far as its relation to the *Prophet* is concerned, we consider the practice of *Sahabah*, because they are the direct students of the *Prophet*. They preserved *Deen* in its words, spirit and practice.

So, let us proceed now to the very topic of *Salat Ul Witr*.

Salat Ul Witr is *sunnah* according to *Jumhur* (the *Malikites*, *Shafites* and *Hanbalites*).

They referred to a few *Ahadith* as follows:

> When a Bedouin asked the Prophet about Mandatory practices, the Prophet said to him: "Five prayers in day and night". He said: "Is there any other requirement of me?" He replied: "No, but if you wish you may pray extra (Nafl) (Bukhari, Muslim).

Muaaz says, the Messenger of *Allah* said,

> *verily Allah has made five prayers mandatory in one day and night (Bukhari, Muslim).*
>
> *Ubadah Ibni Samit refused, a man said that* Witr *is* Wajib *and said to him: "I heard the Messenger of Allah saying five prayers in a day and night. Allah has made a slave [of him] (Ahmad, Abu Dawud).*

Ali said:

> *"Witr is not Hat'm (Fard) like a mandatory prayer, but a sunnah that the Prophet started (Ahmad, Abu Dawud).*
>
> *Ibni Umar used to pray Witr on his camel. So, it means that Witr is not Fard as Fard may not be prayed while riding (Bukhari, Muslim).*

But *Abu Hanifa* said that *Witr* is *Wajib*, neither *Fard* nor *Sunnah*. He referred it to a few *Ahadith* as under:

The Messenger of *Allah* said:

> *"O People of Qur'an! Do Witr because Allah is Witr (one which is odd) and he likes Witr (odd) (Abu Dawud)."*

Here the Commandment gives the concept of *Fard*. But later, the concept of likeness reduced it to a lower level than *Fard* and that is *Wajib*:

Ibni Abbas said the Messenger of *Allah* said:

"Three are made Fard for me, but not for you, Salat Ud Duha, sacrifice an animal (on Eid Day) and Witr (Hakim)."

So, these three were *Fard* for the *Prophet*, not for us. But less than that would be *Wajib*. The only case is that of *Salat Ud Duha*, which is *Nafl*, so we can say that it was *Wajib* for the *Prophet* and less in status for us so that is *Nafl*, but the *Prophet* used to give it due importance. That is why he included the same with other two important deeds.

The Messenger of *Allah* said:

"Verily, Allah has added you a prayer. Beware that is Witr. So, pray it in between Isha and daybreak."

This is narrated by eight *Sahabah*: *Kharijah Ibni Huzafa, Amr Ibnul Aas, Oqbah Ibni Aamir, Ibni Abbas, Abu Basra Al Ghifari, Amr Ibni Shuaib* from his father and he from his grandfather, *Ibni Umar*, and *Abu Saeed Al Khudri*.

Abu Dawud and *Tirmizi* related it from *Kharijah* and *Hakim Saeed* regarding this that this is *Saheeh Ul Isuad*:

The Messenger of *Allah* said;

Witr is Haqq (truth), so whosoever likes to do Witr by five (Rakat) he may do and whosoever likes to do Witr by three, he may do, and whosoever likes to do Witr by one, he may do (Abu Dawud, Nisa'i, Ibni Maja from Abu Ayub).

Buraidah says the Messenger of *Allah* said;

> *Witr is Haqq so whosoever did not do Witr, he is not from amongst us (Ahmad from Buraidah).*

So, in the *Hadith* narrated by eight *Sahabah* the *Prophet* attributed their adding to *Allah* so it should have been *Fard*, but as *Fard* prayers are five in number, its level is lower than those prayers. That is why we say it is *Wajib* and not *Fard*.

Then the *Hadith* of *Abu Ayub* and *Buraidah* said it is *Haqq*, which is synonymous with *Wajib*. Furthermore, in the *hadith* of *Buraidah* the *Prophet* said

> *"One who didn't, he is not from amongst us."*

The *Prophet* usually does not say this for something that is not compulsory.

Now the actual difference is that of the term *Wajib* as to *Jumhur* that is synonymous to *Fard*, but to *Abu Hanifa*, it is lower than *Fard* and higher than *Sunnah*.

Then this prayer is for all those who are bound to pray Friday and *Eidaain*, so men and women both may pray this.

HOW MANY *RAKAT* IS THIS?

The *Malikites* said this is one *Rakat* after the two *Sunnah* of *Isha* separating the *Witr* and *Sunnah* by *Salam* from each other, also this is recommended to recite *Surat Ul Ikhlas, Surat Ul Falaq* and *Surat Un Naas* in these three *Rakat*.

The *Hanbalites* said, one *Rakat* is the recommended practice, but it is also allowed to pray three or more.

The *Shafiites* said its Minimum is one *Rakat* and the Maximum is 11 *Rakat*, but one who wants to pray more than one *Rakat* may intend *Witr* in the last three *Rakat* separating these three by making *Salam* after two *Rakat*, then pray one, as *Ibni Hibban* relates that the *Prophet* used to separate three *Rakat* by making *Salam* after two *Rakat* – and *Muslim* narrated from *Ibni Umar* and *Ibni Abbas* that the Messenger of *Allah* said that *Witr* is one *Rakat* in the end of the night. Also in the *Hadith* of *Abu Ayub*, it is said

"Whosoever wishes to do one Rakat, he may do so."

Also, *Ibni Hibban* relates from *Ibni Abbas* that the *Prophet* did *Witr* by one. *Imam Abu Hanifa* said *Witr* is three *Rakat* without *Salam* in between.

So, first we will quote those narrations, which say that *Witr* is three *Rakat*:

> *Muhammad Ibni Ali Ibni Abdullah Ibni Abbas narrates from his father from his grandfather that the Prophet woke up at night, used Siwak (and made wudu), then he prayed two Rakat, then he slept, then woke up, used Siwak, made wudu, then prayed two Rakat till he prayed six (altogether), then he did Witr with three Rakat and prayed two Rakat (Muslim, Nisa'i).*

> *Yahya Ibnul Jazzar relates from Ibni Abbas that the Messenger of Allah used to pray at night eight Rakat and (used to) do Witr with three and pray two Rakat before Fajr prayer (Nisa'i, Tahawi).*

> *Saeed Ibni Jubair from Ibni Abbas, he said that the Prophet of Allah used to do Witr with three, reciting Surat Ul Ala in first Rakat, Surat Ul Kafirun in the second Rakat and Surat Ul Ikhlas in the third one (Darimi, Tirmizi, Nisa'i, Ibni Maja, Tahawi, Ibni Abi Shaibah and Al Muhalla). Ibni Hajar said "this hadith is Sahih Ul Isnad according to Nawawi."*

Amir Ash Shabi said

> *"I asked Ibni Umar and Ibni Abbas, how did the Prophet pray at night? They both said, "13 Rakat (first, 8 Rakat*

and [then] do Witr with three and two Rakat after Fajr (daybreak) (Tahawi).

Thabit Al Banami said that Anas Ibni Malik told me, O Thabit! Take from me as you cannot take from one much more authentic than I. I have taken it from the Messenger of Allah, he took it from Jibril and Jibril took it from Allah. He said then he led me in Isha then he prayed six Rakat, making Salam after every two Rakat then he did Witr with three making Salam in its end. (Narrated by Ar Royani and Ibni Asakir (Kanzul Ummal, Volume 4).

Imam Abu Hanifa said that Abu Jafar Muhammad al Baqir told us that the Messenger of Allah used to pray in between Salat Ul Isha up to Salat Ul Fajr 13 Rakat, 8 out of it was Nafl, three Rakat Witr and two Rakat (sunnah) of Fajr (Imam Muhammad).

Abu Salamah Ibni Abdur Rahman said I asked Aisha, how did the Prophet pray in Ramadan? She said, the Messenger of Allah used not to pray, in Ramadan or other [month,] more than 11 Rakat. He used to pray four, so don't ask of its beauty and length, then he used to pay four so don't ask of its beauty and length, then used to pray three (Bukhari, Volume 1, Muslim, Volume 1, Nisa'i, Abu Dawud and Ahmad, Volume 6)."

Abdul Aziz Ibni Juraij says,

"I asked Aisha, by what (surah) did the Prophet of Allah pray Witr? She said, he used to pray Surat Ul Ala in first

Rakat, Surat Ul Kafirun in the second and Surat Ul Ikhlas in the third Rakat. Tirmizi said, this hadith is Gharib."

Amrah relates from Aisha that the Messenger of Allah used to pray three Rakat Witr reciting Surat Ul Ala in the first Rakat and in the third one, he used to recite Surat Ul Ikhlas, Surat Ul Falaq and Surat un Nas (Al-Mustadrak, Volume 1)."

Here the second *Rakat* is not mentioned but it is known from other narrations that he used to recite *Surat Ul Kafirun* in the second *Rakat*.

The recitation of three *Surahs* in three *Rakat Witr* is narrated by:

Abdur Rahman Ibni Abza (Nisa'i, Ibni Abi Shaiba, Volume 2).

Ubai Ibni Ka'b (Nisa'i, Tahawi, Ibni Abi Shaiba, Volume 2, Abdur Razaq, Volume 3).

Ali Ibni Abi Talib (Tirmizi, Tahawi, Abdur Razaq, Volume 3).

Abdullah Ibni Abi Aufa (Majma Uz Zawa'id, Volume 2).

Ibni Masud (Majma Uz Zawa'id, Volume 2).

Neman Ibni Bashir (Majma Uz Zawa'id, Volume 2).

Abu Huraira (Majma Uz Zawa'id, Volume 2).

Ibni Umar (Majma Uz Zawa'id, Volume 2).

Imran Ibni Husain (Tahawi Ibni Abi Shaiba, Volume 2, Kanzul-Ummal, Volume I).

Mua'wiyah Ibni Khadeej (Majma Uz Zawa'id, Volume 2).

Then the *Prophet* used to pray three *Rakat Witr* with one *Salam*, as it is in the following narrations:

Sa'd Ibni Hisham said that Aisha told him that the Prophet used not to make Salam in two Rakat of Witr (Nisa'i and Mu'atta of Imam Muhammad).

Hakim in *Mustadrak, Volume 1,* narrated the same practice from same *Sa'd*.

Also, he narrated the same through another narration chain that the *Prophet* used to pray three *Rakat*, making no *Salam*, but in its end, and *Sa'd* said,

"this is the Witr of Umar Ibnul Khattab,"

and from him the *Madinites* took this practice.

Imam Ahmad in his *Musnad, Volume 6,* narrates from *Sa'd Ibni Hisham* the Messenger of *Allah* entered (his) house after he prayed *Isha*, then he prayed two *Rakat*, then he prayed (another) two *Rakat* lengthier than the first two and then he did *Witr* three *Rakat* making no separation (with *Salam*) in these three *Rakat*, then he prayed two *Rakat* in one sitting.

Now the narration of *Muhammad Ibni Ali* mentioned two *Rakat*, then six *Rakat*, then three *Rakat Witr* and then two *Rakat*, which means eight *Rakat Tahajjud*, then three *Witr* and then two *Rakat Sunnat Ul Fajr*.

The *Riwayat* of *Yahya Ibnul Jazzar, Aamir Ash Shabi* from *Ibni Abbas* and *Ibni Umar*, and the *Riwayat* of *Abu Hanifa* from *Abu Jafar* supported this concept.

The *Riwayat* of *Thabit* from *Anas* mentioned six *Rakat* and then *Witr*. The *Riwayat* of *Aisha* mentioned eight *Rakat* and *Witr*. But there is another *Riwayat* of *Aisha* narrated by *Abdullah Ibni Abi Qais*

> "so I asked Aisha, how many Rakat did the Prophet used to perform with Witr? She said, four and three, also six + 3, and 8 + 3, but he was not doing it with more than 13 Rakat, nor with less than 7 Rakat (Abu Dawud, Tahawi)."

So mostly he used to pray 8 + 3, but the narration of 13 means two *Rakat Sunnah* of *Isha* plus eight *Rakat Tahajjud*, and then three *Witr* and where it is mentioned 15 *Rakat* altogether there the two *sunnah* of *Fajr* are added to it in aggregate.

As far as the two *Rakat* after *Witr* in sitting is concerned, so it was either the *Sunnah* of *Fajr*, and he did so due to some excuse and to mention its permissibility in sitting or it was *Nafl* to teach us that to pray *Nafl* to teach us after *Witr* is permissible also.

But all these *Riwayat* clearly mention that *Witr* is three *Rakat* with one *Salam* at its end.

For further clarification, the following *Riwayat* are brought forth:

Abu Hurairah narrates from the *Prophet* that he said:

> "Don't pray Witr with three but with five or seven and don't make it like a Maghreb prayer (Tahawi, Dari Qutni)."

It means that *Salat Ul Witr* in number of *Rakat* is the same as *Salat Ul Maghreb*, so for its distinction you may add to it two or four *Rakat Nafl* beforehand it to make it five or seven.

Ibni Umar relates that the *Prophet* said:

> "*Salat Ul Maghreb* is the *Witr* of day so make the prayer at night and *Witr* as well (Abdur Razaq)."

This resemblance means resemblance in number of *Rakat*, and that this is a prayer having one *Salam* like that of *Salat Ul Maghreb*.

Imam Ahmad related the like of this from *Ibni Umar* as well and *Iraqi* (a critic of *Hadith*) said that its narration chain is authentic.

Aisha narrated from the *Prophet* that he said:

> "*Witr* is three *Rakat* like three of *Maghreb* prayer (Tabrani, Dari Qutni)."

It means with one *Salam*. This *Hadith* has a *Daeef* narrator, but this is all right, as it is just for support, and it is very subject is supported by other *Ahadith*.

Ibni Masud relates that the *Prophet* said:

> *Witr* at night is like the *Witr* of day, i.e., *Salat Ul Maghreb* (Dari Qutni).

These two *Ahadith* i.e., numbers 4 and 5, have been discussed by the critics and they said these two may be the sayings of *Aisha* and *Ibni Masud* and not of the *Prophet*. But we say anything that could not be said or found through an intellectual approach and been said by a *Sahabi* is considered *Marfu* and one of these things is the number and the *Ibadaat*.

So, these *Ahadith* made it very much clear that *Salat Ul Witr* may be prayed as three *Rakat* with one *Salam*.

TA'AMULUS - SAHABAH WAT - TABIEEN

The continuous practice of *Sahabah* and *Tabi'een* is the source to clarify the position of a *Hadith* and practice that has some ambiguity or confusion. There the scholars decide the matter according to this practice and their practice was as follows:

> *Miswar Ibnul Mukhrama said, when we did bury Abu Bakr at night then Umar said, I have not prayed Witr yet, so we made rows behind him and he led us in three Rakat and did not make Salam. But in its end (Tahawi, Ibni Abi Shaiba, Volume 1 and Abdur Razaq, Volume 3).*

Hakim narrated in *Al Mustadrak, Volume 1* from *Sa'd Ibni Hisham* that the Messenger of *Allah* used to pray *Witr* three *Rakat*, making no *Salam* but in its end – and this is the *Witr* of *Umar Ibnul Khattab*.

Ibrahim Nakha'e relates from *Umar Ibnul Khattab* to say:

> *"I don't like to miss three Rakat Witr and have red cattle [in exchange]."*

Red cattle (camels) were the most valuable property of *Arabs* at that time.

> *Makhul said that Umar Ibnul Khattab prayed* Witr *three Rakat without Salam in between (Ibni Abi Shaiba, Volume 2).*

It was said to *Hasan Al Basri* that *Ibni Umar* makes *Salam* after two *Rakat* of *Witr*, so he said but *Umar* (his father) was a greater *Faqih* than him (meaning he was not doing so) (*Mustadrak*). Also, we said before that *Ibni Umar* related from the *Prophet* that *Salat Ul Maghreb* is the *Witr* of day so one makes the prayer of night *Witr* as well (to pray three *Rakat* like that of *Maghreb*).

> *Zazan Abu Umar said that Ali used to pray like this (three Rakat) (Ibni Abi Shaiba, Volume 2).*

> *Ibni Masud said that Witr is three Rakat like the Witr of daytime i.e., Salat Ul Maghreb (Tahawi, Abdur Razaq, Volume 2, Mu'atta of Muhammad, Tabrani).*

> *Alqama relates from Ibni Masud that Witr may be three Rakat at least (Mu'atta of Muhammad).*

Uqba Ibni Muslim said,

> "*I asked Ibni Umar about Witr, so he said, "do you know the Witr of day time? I said, yes, Salat Ul Maghreb. He said, you spoke the truth and said good (Tahawi).*"

> *Abu Mansur said, I asked Ibni Abbas about Witr, so he said, "three Rakat" (Tahawi).*

Anas said, Witr is three Rakat and he used to do three (Tahawi and Ibni Abi Shaiba, Volume 2).

Ata said from Ibni Abbas that Witr is the like of Salat Ul Maghreb (Mu'atta of Muhammad).

Hasan said,

"Ubai Ibni Ka'b used to pray Witr three Rakat, making no Salam but in the end like Maghreb (Abdur Razaq, Volume 3)."

Abu Ghalib said that Abu Umama used to pray Witr three Rakat (Tahawi, Ibni Abi Shaiba, Volume 2).

Abu Yahya says that Ibni Abbas and Miswar Ibni Makhrama were talking after Isha till the red glow on the horizon appeared then Ibni Abbas slept and could not wake up but with the voices of people of Zaura (close to Medina) so he said to his companions, do you think I can pray three Rakat (Witr), two sunnah of Fajr and the Fajr prayer (two Rakat Fard) before sunrise? They said, yes, and this was in the last part of Fajr (Tahawi).

Alqama said that Witr is three Rakat (Ibni Abi Shaiba, Volume 2).

Ibrahim (Nakha'e) said, there is no Witr less than three Rakat. (Ibni Abi Shaiba, Volume 2).

Abu Ishaq said, the companions of Ali and Ibni Masud used not to make Salam in (after) two Rakat of Witr. (Ibni Abi Shaiba).

Hasan al Basri said, the Muslims agreed upon unanimously that Witr is three Rakat with no Salam, but in its end. (Ibni Abi Shaiba, Volume 2).

Qasim Ibni Muhammad says, we saw people since we attained the age of puberty, praying three Rakat Witr and this is a relaxed practice, and I think that there is no sin in any practice of Witr [meaning if someone prays it after two or four Nafl or without this] (Bukhari, Volume 1).

Abu Khalida says, I asked Abul Aaliya about Witr, so he said that the companions of Prophet Muhammad taught us that Witr is like salat al Maghreb. But we recite in the third Rakat (while there is no Fard Qira'at in the third Rakat of Maghreb), so this is the Witr of night and this [Maghreb] is the Witr of day (Tahawi).

Imam Tahawi narrated from Abuz Zinad that Umar Ibni Abdul Aziz established the practice of Witr three Rakat as the jurists told him, making no Salam, but in its end.

Also, *Tahawi* said from *Abu Zinad* that three *Rakat Witr* without *Salam* in between is the practice of the *Fuqaha-I-Sab'a* (seven well-known and authentic jurists).

These *Fuqaha* are *Saeed Ibnul Musayyib, Urwah Ibniz Zubair, Qasim Ibni Muhammad Abu Bakr Ibni Abdur Rahman, Kharijah Ibni Zaid, Ubaid Ullah Ibni Abdullah, Sulaiman Ibni Yasar,* and some other pious and virtuous Jurists, maybe they will have a little bit of a difference of an opinion, but most them agreed with this practice.

> *Saeed Ibni Jubair relates from Ibni Abbas, Witr is seven or five Rakat while three Rakat is Butaira and I dislike Butaira (Tahawi, Abdur Razaq, Volume 3).*

> *Saeed Ibnul Musayyib said from Aisha that she said, "Witr is seven or five Rakat and three Rakat is Butaira" (Ibni Abi Shaiba, Volume 2).*

As we mentioned before that the recommended practice is to pray a few *Rakat Nafl* before *Witr* so to pray *Witr* only is *Butaira*. This is derived from *Batara* which means

"to cut off"

or

"to amputate",

and that deprives it of beauty, so to pray three *Witr* only is to make it less beautiful as *Ibni Masud* said,

"I dislike it."

Ibrahim relates from *Ibni Masud* that he said,

> *"One Rakat cannot suffice [as far as prayer is concerned]."*

THE *RIWAYAAT* AND ANALYSIS

As we said that *Jumhur* used the word *Wajib* as a synonym of *Fard*. But *Abu Hanifa* used *Wajib* for something lower than *Fard* and higher than *sunnah*. That's why about *Witr*, *Jumhur* says that this is *Sunnah* while *Abu Hanifa* said,

"This is Wajib."

Regarding the night prayer of the *Prophet* there are a few *Riwayat*:

The *Riwayat* of *Ibni Abbas* –

His son *Ali*, his students *Yahya Ibnul Jazzar*, *Saeed Ibni Jubair* and his liberated slave *Kuraib*, narrate from *Ibni Abbas* that the *Prophet* prayed *Witr* 3 *Rakat*, when *Ibni Abbas* spent night in the house of the *Prophet*.

Bukhari and *Muslim* narrate a *Riwayat* from *Kuraib* that *Ibni Abbas* said that the *Prophet* prayed two *Rakat* then two, then two, then two, then two, then two and then he did *Witr*. So this then he did *Witr* (*Autar*) may be explained in the light of all those other *Riwayat* that he added a third *Rakat* to the last two mentioned by him, i.e., the sixth in number, so eventually the result is that the *Prophet* prayed 10 *Rakat Nafl* and then 3 *Witr*, because the same *Kuraib* narrated from *Ibni Abbas* 3 *Rakat Witr* of the *Prophet* as narrated by *Tahawi* in the same way *Imam Muslim* relates from *Zaid Ibni Khalid Al Juhani* six times two *Rakat* and then *Autara*, which that also means that then he made it *Witr* by adding a third *Rakat* to the last two.

Almost ten *Sahaba* narrated that the *Prophet* used to pray 3 *Rakat Witr*.

Imam Bukhari narrated from *Saeed Ibni Jubair* and he from *Ibni Abbas*,

> *"I came to the Prophet, he prayed 4 Rakat, then he slept, then woke up so I came and stood to his left side, but he put me to his right side and prayed 5 Rakat, then prayed two Rakat."*

These five *Rakat* means he prayed 2 *Rakat Nafl*, then 3 *Witr* and then two *Rakat sunnah* of *Fajr*. And what *Abu Dawud* related,

> *"He prayed 5 Rakat and did not sit in between,"*

meaning that he did not sit between two *Nafl* and 3 *Witr*. This is supported by the *Fatwa* of *Ibni Abbas* that

> *"I do not like to pray Witr alone, but [prefer] to put a few Nafl before it."*

Now, the common thing in these *Riwayat* is that the *Prophet* used to pray *Witr* 3 *Rakat*, even though his *Nafl* before it differed in number.

The *Riwayat* of *Abu Ayub* – In his *Riwayat Abu Ayub* relates from the *Prophet*,

> "*so whosoever likes to do Witr with five, he can do it, and whosoever wishes to do Witr with three, he can do it and whosoever wants to do Witr with one he can do it. (Abu Dawud, Nisa'i, Ibni Maja).*"

> *Regarding this last part of "one" Hafiz Ibni Hajar said that Imam Hakim, Zuhali, Dari Qutni and Bayhaqi said, "This is the saying of Abu Ayub (At Talkhees Ul Habeer, Volume 2)."*

As *Dari Qutni* related this *Hadith*,

> "*Witr is Wajib so whosoever wants so he may do Witr with three.*"

Then *Ibni Hajar* said that the narrators of this *Riwayat* are authentic, while *Imam Nisa'i* related this:

> "*So whosoever likes to do Witr with 7, he can do so; and whosoever wants to do Witr with 5 he can do so; whosoever to do Witr with one he can do so; and whosoever wants he can do it with indication.*"

So, we can say that there is *Idtiraab* in this *Riwayat* and even there is the concept of indication and nobody said that indication is enough in *Witr* prayer.

The *Hadith* of *Ibni Umar*: *Bukhari* and *Muslim* narrated from *Ibni Umar* that someone asked the *Prophet* of *Allah* about prayer at night. He said,

> "Prayer at night is two two Rakat, so when someone has a fear of dawn break he may pray one Rakat [and it will] make odd for him what he has prayed."

Also, *Abu Mijlaz* related from *Ibni Umar* and *Ibni Abbas* that the Messenger of *Allah* said,

> "Witr is one Rakat at night."

This *Riwayat* of *Abu Mijlaz* is not a different *Hadith*, but a part of the previous *Hadith* of *Ibni Umar* as a narration by *Ibni Maja* supporting it where it is said:

> "Prayer at night is two and two, and Witr is one Rakat before dawn."

> Then Hafiz Ibni Hajar said that this Hadith is not particular in separation of this one Rakat so it means: "pray one Rakat added to two [previous] Rakat (Fathul Bari, Volume 2)."

This third *Rakat* is making those two an odd one, and *Witr* means odd.

Ibni Umar already related a *Hadith* that

> "Salat Ul Maghreb is the Witr of daytime, so make the prayer at night a Witr (odd) as well."

Now, his mention of *Salat Ul Maghreb* as *Witr* proves the resemblance of these two prayers to one another.

Also, it is very well known from the *Prophet's Hadith* where he said:

When you are afraid (of daybreak) then do Ietar with one.
It will make odd what you prayed.

It means add one more to the last two *Rakat*, which will make it odd and *Witr*. So ultimately it is 3 *Rakat*.

The *Hadith* of *Ummi Salmah*:

Yahya Ibnul Jazzar related from her that the Messenger of Allah used to pray 11 Rakat at night but when he became older and weak he did Witr with 7 (Nisa'i, Tirmizi).

This *Hadith* is the like of the *Hadith* of *Aisha*.

Yahya Ibnul Jazzar narrated from *Ibni Abbas* that the Messenger of *Allah* used to pray 3 *Rakat* at night and did *Witr* with 3 *Rakat*. So, she titled all 7 *Rakat* as *Witr*, but *Imam Tirmizi* relates from *Ishaq Ibni Ibrahim* that it means that the *Prophet* used to pray 13 *Rakat* with *Witr* at night, so the whole prayer is called *Witr*.

Maqsim narrated from *Ummi Salmah* that the *Prophet* used to do *Witr* with 5 and 7, not making separation in between by *Salam*. But *Imam Nisa'i* has mentioned that *Maqsim* sometimes narrated the same directly from *Ibni Abbas*, sometimes through *Ibni Abbas*, and sometimes he attributes this to *Aisha* and *Maimunah*, that *Witr* is 7 but no less than five

Rakat. So, *Imam Nisa'i* said that the very chain of this *Hadith* has *Idtiraab* (confusion), or it means that he used to pray two or four *Rakat* before 3 *Witr* and

"not separating [it] with Salam or Kalam"

means that by this *Salam* she means the usual greeting, as this is supported by and

"no speaking"

or this

"no Salam"

means he was not making it loudly in order not to disturb the sleep of his family, as this concept is mentioned in the *Hadith* of *Aisha*.

The *Hadith* of *Aisha* –

Muslim narrates from *Sa'd Ibni Hisham* that when he asked *Aisha* regarding the *Witr* of the *Prophet*, she said,

> *"He used to pray 9 Rakat not sitting, but in the eighth one, so he used to remember Allah, praise him, invoke him, then stand without Salam, then pray the 9th one, then sit, remembering Allah, praising him, invoking him, then making Salam, making it heard to us, then praying two Rakat in sitting so these are 11 Rakat, my son! But when he was aged and fat he used to do Witr with 7 Rakat and used to do in two Rakat as he did in the first two, so there are 9 Rakat, O my son!"*

So, some scholars said that the *Prophet* used to pray 9 *Rakat Witr* sitting in the eighth one and making *Salam* after the 9th and when he was aged, he prayed 7 *Rakat*, sitting in the 6th one only and making *Salam* in the 7th one.

But we say that *Nisa'i, Imam Muhammad* in *Mu'atta, Tahawi, Ibni Hazm* in *Al-Muhalla, Volume 2, Ibni Abi Shaibah* in *Volume 2, Imam Hakim* in *Volume 1, Dari-Qutni* and *Bayhaqi* in *Volume 3*, narrated this *Hadith* in which it is said that the *Prophet* used to do 3 *Rakat Witr* making no *Salam* but in its end.

Also, *Imam Ahmad* narrated it in *Volume 6*, that the *Prophet* entered his house, prayed two *Rakat*, then two *Rakat* longer than the first two, then prayed 3 *Witr* making no separation in between (by *Salam*) then prayed two *Rakat* in sitting.

Now from this *Riwayat* of *Aisha*, we know a few things: The *Prophet* used to pray 11 *Rakat* at night; out of these there was *Witr* and two *Rakat* of these 11 he prayed after *Witr*. He used to sit after every two *Rakat*. *Salat Ul Witr* was 3 *Rakat*. He used to sit after 2 *Rakat* in *Witr* without making *Salam*, standing at the third one and completing it.

He was praying two *Rakat* after *Witr* in sitting.

> *The second Riwayat is that of Urwah from Aisha as narrated by Muslim that the Prophet used to pray 11 Rakat at night, making Witr with one Rakat and when he finished it he used to lie on his right side until the Mu'azzin came to him, then he used to pray 2 Rakat lightly. In another Riwayat of him it is mentioned that he used to lie on*

his right side after the two Rakat of Fajr till the Mu'azzin comes to him for Iqama (Muslim).

Also in another *Hadith* of *Urwah*, it is mentioned that the *Prophet* used to pray 13 *Rakat* doing *Witr* with five not sitting but in its end.

In a narration of *Imam Tahawi* from *Urwah* it is said that he used to pray 13 *Rakat* at night, then pray 2 *Rakat* when he heard *A'zan*.

And *Muslim* mentioned in one narration of him that he used to pray 13 *Rakat* including the two *Sunnah* of *Fajr*.

So, all these may be explained that he used to sit after every two *Rakat* as that is the procedure in prayer and that he used to pray *Witr* 3 *Rakat* as *Aisha* the authentic source regarding his *Witr* said in her *Mutawatir* sayings. So, the meaning of *Autara Bi Wahidatin* is that he made the last two *Rakat* an odd by adding another one *Rakat* to it, and it is mentioned that he used not to sit in between means sitting after *Salam*, but stand to another two right after *Salam*, as *Ibni Abbas* relates *that he prayed with the Prophet 8 Rakat together and 7 Rakat together (Muslim).*

This is regarding *Zuhr* and *Asr*, and regarding *Maghreb* and *Isha*. So, it does not mean that he was not sitting in between, but he was not sitting a long after *Salam* from one prayer and starting the other one.

The *Riwayat* of *Ibni Abi Shaibah* said that he used to do *Witr* with one *Rakat* and used to speak between two *Rakat* and one *Rakat*, so it means he used to make it odd by adding one *Rakat* to it, and his speaking was in between the *Witr* and the two *Rakat* he used to pray after *Witr*.

Abu Salmah Ibni Abdur Rahman, Amrah Bint Abdur Rahman, Abdullah Ibni Oais and *Abdul Aziz Ibni Juraij*: all of them related 3 *Rakat Witr* of the *Prophet* from *Aisha*.

Yahya Ibnul Jazzar, Aswad Ibni Oais and *Masruq Ibni Ajda* have not expressed the number of *Rakat* from *Aisha* but it is known from the other *Riwayat* of *Aisha* that the number is 3.

Hafiz Ibni Hajar related a saying of *Hafiz Ibnus Salah* that

> "We don't know from all these Riwayat regarding Witr that the Prophet ever prayed one Rakat Witr (At Talkhees, Volume 2)."

Even though *Hafiz* himself related the *Riwayat* of *Kuraib* that he did *Witr* with one, but we already explained it.

Then the *Ijma'* of *Sahabah* in the time of *Umar* was on 3 *Rakat* in *Ramadan*.

Also, the same was the practice of *Muslims* in the time of *Ali* in *Ramadan*; even though those who did not take into consideration the *Riwayat* of 20 *Rakat Taraweeh* have taken the *Riwayat* of 3 *Rakat Witr* as is.

HOW TO PRAY THESE THREE *RAKAT*

1. *Qadah* or sitting after two *Rakat* and then to stand for the third one.

Imam Tirmizi related from *Fazl Ibni Abbas* that the Messenger of *Allah* said:

> *(A unit of) prayer is wo two Rakat [with] Tashah'hud in each two Rakat.*

Ibni Majah relates:

> *Prayer at night is two [Rakat].*

Now the *Riwayat* of *Tirmizi* said what is called *Salat* may be *Fard*, *Wajib*, *Sunnah* or *Nafl*, etc. It may be two *Rakat* at least, so there is no concept of one *Rakat* and it also means that there will be a sitting and *Tashah'hud* after every two *Rakat* as well, while the *Riwayat* of *Ibni Majah* says that prayer at night is two two *Rakat*, which means it is better to pray it in pairs even though one can pray that in eight *Rakat* unit as well. But still he must make *Tashah'hud* after every two *Rakat*.

Tabrani related from *Ummi Salmah* that the *Prophet* said:

In every two Rakat there is Tashah'hud and Salam also on the Messengers and on those who followed them from amongst the righteous slaves of Allah.

It means *At-Tahiyyat*.

Yes, in this *Riwayat* there is *Ali Ibni Zaid*, the scholars differed in their opinions regarding him. Some said he is authentic, but others disagreed. But then the critics said that in such a case the first opinion is preferred.

Muslim related from *Aisha* that the *Prophet* said:

In every two Rakat there is At-Tahiyyat.

Bukhari and *Muslim* narrated from *Ibni Umar* that a man asked the *Prophet* about prayer at night. He told him,

"Prayer at night is two two Rakat."

Also, *Imam Muslim* narrated that *Ibni Umar* said, *"two two"* means to make *Salam* after every two *Rakat*.

So, *Salam* means either the known way of going out of prayer or the Salam mentioned there in *At-Tahiyyat*, as it is said in the aforesaid *Riwayat* of *Ummi Salmah* and *Aisha*.

All these *Riwayat* mean that there is no concept of one *Rakat Witr*. Yes, if someone said that this is a *Hadith* that:

Witr is one *Rakat* at night, we say that this is like a *Hadith* where it is said that *Hajj* (pilgrimage to *Mecca*) is *Arafah* while *Hajj* is not *Arafah* only but there are other *Manasik* also. But the importance of *Arafah* is mentioned here that it makes the *Hajj* a *Hajj*; the same is true of this other *Hadith* that this one *Rakat* makes the night prayer a *Witr*.

2. *Qunut* literally means obedience and submission and technically it is the *Dua* recited inside the prayer. Then this *Dua* is of two types:

   a) *Qunut Un Nawazil,* which is to be recited on special occasions when *Muslims* are brutalized and suffering atrocities. This is recommended according to the *Hanafites, Shafiites,* and *Hanbalites*. Imam *Tahawi* said that this is the discretion of the *Khalifa* to decide whether it is to be recited or not.

According to *Hanbalites* it is to be recited in *Fajr* only. In other saying they said in every *Fard* prayer except Friday prayer as the *Dua* is already been made in *Khutbah*.

The *Shafiites* said in *Fajr* prayer only while according to *Hanafites* it could be recited in any *Jahri* prayer it may be recited loudly after *Ruku*.

Then *Shafiites* and *Hanbalites* may raise their heads and say *Aamin* loudly, but according to *Hanafites* they may leave their heads hanging and say *Aamin* secretly like that in *Khutbah*. Then the *Shafiites* and *Hanbalites* said these are the *Aadaab* of *Dua*, as in this *Hadith* –

> *"When you invoke Allah, do invoke with by the inside of your palms and not the back side of it and when you are done then touch your face with it (Abu Dawud, Ibni Maja)."*

Also, *Abu Dawud* related from *Sa'ib Ibni Yazeed* and he related from his father that the *Prophet*, whenever he made *Dua*, raised his hands and touched his face with it.

But the *Hanafites* said that it is not mentioned anywhere that he raised his hands for *Dua* inside the prayer, as *Haitham* related through *Tabrani* from *Muhammad Ibni Yahya Al Aslami* that *Ibni Zubair* saw one man raising his hands for *Dua* in prayer, and when he was done, he said to him that the Messenger of *Allah* used not to raise his hands but after prayer (*Majma Uz Zawa'id, Volume 10*).

Sayuti also related the same that the Messenger of *Allah* used not to raise his hands but after prayer (*Majma Uz Zawa'id, Volume 10*).

b) *Al Qunut Ud Da'im*, which is recited always. The *Malikites* and *Shafiites* said this is to be recited in *Fajr* prayer before *Ruku*, but still it is allowed after *Ruku* also. The words of that *Qunut* are the words of *Hanafites* in *Witr*, but to *Shafiites* the *Qunut* may be after *Ruku*, while according to the *Malikites* this is *Makruh* to recite *Qunut* except in *Salat Fajr*. According to the *Malikites* it may be recited slowly. The words of that *Qunut* are the words related by *Umar* and his son *Abdullah* and that is –

"*Allahumma Inna Nastaeenuka...*"

As *Abu Dawud* narrated for *Khalid Ibni Imran* that the *Prophet* was making *Dua* against *Mudar* (a tribe) when *Jibril* came to him and indicated to him to be silent. He said,

> "*O Muhammad! Allah has not sent you to vilify or to curse but He (Allah, sent you as a Marcy – not for you is the decision (but for Allah,).*"

then he taught him the *Qunut*.

Also, the *Sahabah* unanimously practiced this *Qunut*.

All those who pray *Witr* may recite it slowly and if he forgot he may not come back from *Ruku* and make *Sajdah-I-Sahu* in the end.

According to *Shafiites* the *Sunnah Qunut* is –

"Allahumahidna feeman…"

And may be recited in the second *Rakat* of *Fajr* prayer after *Ruku*, but the *Imam* may recite it in the form of first person plural.

Anas Ibni Malik said the *Prophet* used to recite *Qunut* in *Fajr* till he left this world *(Ahmad),* and *Umar* used to recite *Qunut* in *Fajr*.

Also, it is said that they used to raise their hands but upside down and not touching their faces. In the words of *Dua*, the *Imam* will recite loudly and the follower may say

"Aamin"

while after that, in words of *Zikr*, he may recite slowly. But if the followers are far behind then their *Imam* than they may recite it on their own. This is also recommended to combine both *Qunut*.

According to *Hanafites* and *Hanbalites Qunut* is in the third *Rakat*, but according to *Hanbalites* it is after *Ruku*, but still allowed before it as well as *Ibni Masud* said the *Prophet* recited it after *Ruku (Muslim)* and *Ibni Maja* narrates from *Anas* that we used to recite before and sometime after *Ruku* also in *Fajr*. *Hanbalites* also said that there is no *Qunut* in *Fajr*, but in circumstances.

Then *Imam Shafi* says that *Qunut* may be recited in *Witr* in the last half of *Ramadan*.

According to *Hanafites* the *Qunut* is after *Qira'at* in the third *Rakat* before *Ruku*. After *Qira'at* he may say *Takbeer* and raise his hand as he does when making *Tahreemah* then put his hand beneath his belly button as he does at the time of *Qira'at*. Yes, in circumstances he may recite *Qunut Nazilah* after *Ruku* in any *Jahri* prayer.

Umar, Ali, Ibni Abbas Ubai Ibni Ka'b Ibni Masud, all said that the *Prophet* used to recite *Qunut* in *Witr* before *Ruku*.

Imam Bukhari also relates that *Asim* said,

> *I asked Anas. He said Qunut is there. I said, "Before Ruku or after?" He said, "Before it." I said that Mr. So-and-so told me that you said after. He said, "He told a lie, indeed. The Prophet recited Qunut after Ruku only one month."*

Then the narration of *Anas* as *Haithami* related that the *Prophet* recited *Qunut* till death, *Abu Bakr* till death and *Umar* till death, it means in *Witr*. And the words narrated by *Ahmad* and *Bazzar* that the *Prophet* used to recite *Qunut* in *Fajr* till he left the world, it means in circumstances.

Nisa'i and *Ibni Majah,* narrated from *Ubai Ibni Ka'b, Dari Qutni* and *Ibni Abi Shaiba* from *Ibni Masud, Abu Naeem* from *Ibni Abbas* and *Tabrani* from *Ibni Umar* related that the *Prophet* recited *Qunut* before *Ruku*.

> *Imam Tirmizi relates in Kitab Ul Ilal, Volume 2, from Ibni Masud that the Prophet used to recite Qunut before Ruku. Aswad said, I stayed with Umar for six months; he used*

to recite *Qunut* before *Ruku (Muhammad's Kitab Ul Hajjah, Volume 1)*.

TAKBEER FOR QUNUT:

Ibni Abdul Barr related a *Hadith* from *Ummi Abd*, the mother of *Ibni Masud*, when he sent him to watch the *Witr* of the *Prophet* at home. She said that the *Prophet* recited *Surat Ul Aala* in the first *Rakat*, *Surat Ul Kafirun* in the second *Rakat*, and *Surat Ul Ikhlas* in the third *Rakat*, then he said *Takbeer* and recited *Qunut*, then he said *Takbeer* and made *Ruku*.

Ibni Abi Shaiba related from *Aswad* that *Ibni Masud* used to raise his hands at the time of *Qunut* in *Witr (Musannaf, Volume 2)*.

Also, *Imam Bukhari* in his book *Raful Yadain* related the same practice of *Ibni Masud*. Also, he related the like this from *Abu Uthman* that *Umar* used to raise his hands at *Qunut*.

Ibrahim An Nakha'e said that *Qunut* in *Witr* is *Wajib* in *Ramadan* and other months as well before *Ruku*, so when you go to *Qunut*, say *Takbeer* and when you go to *Ruku*, say *Takbeer* as well *(Kitab Ul Aathar, Volume 1, Kitab Ul Hujjah, Volume 1)*.

Imam Muhammad said this we practice and he may raise hands as he does in *Tahreemah* then put it (beneath the navel) and make *Dua*. This is the stand of *Abu Hanifa*. It is logical and reasonable to separate the *Qira'at* and *Qunut* in words and practice, so the word is *Takbeer* and practice is to raise hands.

Putting hands beneath the belly button is reasonable as well as whenever there is any *Zikr* or *Dua* when standing in prayer; then one may put hands like this if not known otherwise from the practice of the

Prophet or *Sahabah*. The best example of this is *Salat Ul Janazah*, and *Umar* disliked raising hands like in *Dua* when he recited *Qunut,* as related by *Al Haithami in Al Majma, Volume 2.*

Yes, in the chain of this narration there is *Shahr Ibnul Hashab* about whom *Ahmed, Abu Zur'a, Ibni Mueen* and *Abu Hatam* said

"not authentic,"

but *Ayub* and *Ibni Adi* said

"authentic."

This is what we explained only for academic purposes as whatever explanation regarding *Ibadat* is given by the authentic *Mujtahidin* and *Imams*, especially by the well-known four *Imams* of *Ahlus Sunnat* is appreciated even though the *Muqallidin* may follow their own *Imam*. This is reasonable, logical and very close to give one stability.

WHAT IS *ITIKAF?*

The word *Itikaf* is used in the *Holy Quran* in different forms such as A*akifun* or *Al Aakifeen*. Literally, it means confinement to a specific thing or place, or retreat and seclusion, while technically it means to confine oneself for some time to a *Masjid* to stay there to worship or at least to withdraw oneself from worldly business.

This practice of seclusion is also common in religion, and even the *Meccans* and the idolaters of the *Arabian Peninsula* used to perform the same practice for a few days annually or periodically.

Prophet Muhammad used to perform *Itikaf* even before receiving the message. He was in seclusion in the cave of *Hira* when he received the message for the first time. While coming back from the city of *Ta'if*, he again performed this practice as Messenger in that same cave.

The *Prophet* used to fast in *Mecca* even before the fasting in *Ramadan* became mandatory.

Upon his migration to *Medina*, when fasting in *Ramadan* became mandatory he used to perform *Itikaf* in the last 10 days of *Ramadan* in the *Masjid*. In the last year of his life, he did it for 20 days and nights which was considered an indication that he would not live until the next *Ramadan*.

Itikaf is a type of solitude and meditation to reach a state of mental tranquil and spiritual peace, and to clean, purify and sanctify one's inner self.

When one becomes secluded and withdrawn from worldly business in a place of worship, he will be thinking of his Creator and will also feel a connection with his Creator, which will result in mental peace.

Performing *Itikaf* is *Sunnah Kifa'I*, which means it was the practice of the *Prophet*, and that at least one individual from each community must perform it. Otherwise, on the *Day of Judgment* the entire community would be held accountable for not performing *Itikaf*. One may perform a *Nafl* type of *Itikaf* in a *Masjid* for one or two days, or even for an hour according to *Imam Shafi*, *Imam Yusuf*, and *Imam Muhammad*.

Itikaf should be in a *Masjid* where the five daily prayers are held and prayed, and it is recommended that Friday prayer also be prayed there. However, if Friday prayer is not held at that *Masjid*, he may travel to another nearby *Masjid*, but should not waste time outside the *Masjid* while in *Itikaf* (according to the *Hanafi* School).

Imam Ahmad says it must be in a *Masjid* where the five daily prayers are performed, and *Imam Malik* and *Imam Shafi* allow *Itikaf* in any *Masjid*.

One who is in *Itikaf* must not go out of *Masjid* but for a reasonable cause such as using the bathroom if it is outside of the *Masjid*, or to the kitchen if that is outside as well, as these are unavoidable needs. To travel outside of the *Masjid* without reasonable cause would break one's *Itikaf*. According to the *Hanafi* School, one may make it up next time.

Women may also perform *Itikaf*, but in their homes at their specified prayer areas.

For *Itikaf*, all *Masjids* are equal, but if someone gave a pledge to *Allah* that he will do *Itikaf* in *Haram Makki*, or *Haram Madani*, or in *Baitul Maqdas*, then he is bound to do it where he said.

The prerequisites of *Itikaf* are *Islam*, sanity, maturity, intention, fasting, to be pure and clean from menses and bleeding after childbirth and from *Janabat*, and to be in *Masjid* (in case of men).

In *Itikaf*, any type of worship of *Allah* is recommended. These include recitation of the *Holy Quran*, remembrance of *Allah*, asking for forgiveness, the study of religious literature, and the avoidance of useless talk and useless actions.

The feeling experienced in *Itikaf* cannot be generalized for everyone, since everyone may experience a different feeling. However, in brief, *Itikaf* brings one mental tranquility, a feeling of self-control, and a connection to *Allah*.

The *Prophet* said whosoever performs *Itikaf* for one day for the sake of *Allah*, *Allah* will put 3 trenches between him and the hellfire, and every trench will have the distance between the heavens and the earth.

ZAKAT

Zakat is a mandatory financial rite, and one of the five pillars of *Islam*. It must be paid by anyone who owns certain kinds of wealth or valuables whose value is at least equal to the limit of *Nisab*.

Nisab means the minimum amount fixed by *Islamic Shariah* for certain kinds of wealth and valuables.

TERMS AND CONDITIONS

I. *Zakat*-able assets must be at least equivalent to *Nisab*.

II. *Zakat*-able assets at least to the limit of *Nisab* must be in the ownership of a person for one lunar year.

ZAKAT-ABLE ASSETS AND ITS *NISAB*

A. **GOLD:**

The *Nisab* for gold is 3 oz. or 100 g.

B. **SILVER:**

The *Nisab* for silver is 21 oz. or 700 g.

C. **CASH:**

The *Nisab* for cash is an equivalent to the value of the *Nisab* of silver. The evaluation based on silver was the practice of all the *Sahabahs*, *Imams*, and Rulers, therefore most *Muslims* must pay *Zakat*. Since the price of silver is less than that of gold, it is easier for larger number of people to contribute.

D. **MERCHANDISE AND INVENTORIES:**

The *Nisab* for merchandise and inventories is the same as the *Nisab* for cash.

Note: Stocks and shares are considered the same as cash and inventories. However, tools, equipment and machinery used in business are excluded from *Zakat* deduction. This means they are not *Zakat*-able.

IMPORTANT ISSUES IN *ZAKAT*

1. If a person owns wealth or the above-mentioned valuables or merchandise in an amount less than *Nisab*, he is not bound to pay *Zakat*.

2. If a person owns *Nisab*, but it suddenly falls below the *Nisab* limit, then the due date for *Zakat* is delayed for one year from the day when it reaches the *Nisab* limit again.

3. A person may fix his own due date for *Zakat* payment; however, it must be based on the lunar calendar and that date will be his due date for payment every year. For example, a person who fixed the first of Ramadan as his or her due date shall use this date to calculate his or her *Zakat* every year.

4. A person must pay *Zakat* on all his/her owned assets on this due date and not on just the basis of his/her earnings.

5. If a person's wealth fluctuates during the year but he has been the owner of *Nisab* for the whole year, and his wealth never dropped below the level of *Nisab*, he/she may pay *Zakat* for all

the owned wealth on the due date. This is because keeping track of every single increase and decrease during the year is not practical.

6. According to *Imam Abu Hanifa*, *Zakat* is not a wealth tax but a type of worship (*Ibadat*). Therefore, a minor or an insane individual who possesses wealth is not bound to pay *Zakat*. However, *Imam Malik, Shafi* and *Ahmed* state that the individual's guardian must pay *Zakat* on that wealth.

7. There is no *Zakat* on land or homes if they are not for business purposes (e.g., shops, restaurants, business properties, etc.)

8. All due loans are to be dropped from the assets and then *Zakat* is to be paid from the rest.

9. All jewelry other than gold and silver, no matter how precious and valuable, is not *Zakat*-able. However, this exemption is not valid if it is owned for business purposes.

10. According to *Imam Abu Hanifa*, *Zakat* is mandatory on all and any form of gold and silver used by women. However, *Imam Shafi* and *Imam Ahmed* state that there is no *Zakat* on gold and silver that a woman is using.

11. If a person owns more than one type of a *Zakat*-able item, it is not equal to *Nisab* if evaluated separately. However, if they collectively exceed the level of *Nisab*, then the items are *Zakat*-able.

12. If a person has lent money or any *Zakat*-able item to another person and the debtor never denies repaying his creditor, then *Zakat* is to be paid for that wealth as well.

13. A creditor cannot ask a debtor to accept the amount owed as *Zakat* even though the debtor is eligible to receive *Zakat*. The intention for *Zakat* and payment at the same time is a must. If the creditor wishes to benefit the debtor, he/she should give the amount to the debtor physically and then ask him/her to repay the same back to him for the amount he owes him.

14. *Zakat* must be given to those eligible as mentioned in verse 60, chapter 9 of *Surah Taubah*,

"Verily, Sadaqat (the mandatory ones) are only for the Fuqara (poor people who have nothing and ask for nothing); and Masakin (poor people who have very little, and they are asking and begging); and the employees collecting Zakat; and to attract the hearts of those who have been inclined towards Islam; and to free the captives; and for those in debt (for a legitimate cause); and (for those) in the path/cause of Allah (who fight a holy war); and for the wayfarer (a traveler who is cut off from everything), a duty imposed by Allah. And Allah is All-Knower, All-Wise."

Note: All these people mentioned must be *Muslims*.

All prominent *Fuqaha* (scholars of *Islamic Shariah* who are considered an authority in matters related to *Shariah*) have *not* generalized the words *"in the path/cause of Allah"*

to mean that *Zakat* is payable for the burial of dead *Muslims*, the construction of a mosque, hospital, road, bridge, or purchasing land for something, etc. These are the collective responsibilities of the *Muslim Ummah*, and for those who are rich. Since *Zakat* must be a transfer of ownership and possession of *Zakat* money to the afore-mentioned people.

Only *Allamah Kasani* of the *Hanafi* School of Thought generalized it to that meaning, but all the other scholars hold that had that been the case, then *Allah* would not have explicitly mentioned the list of eight categories eligible for *Zakat* in detail.

If *Allah* had said,

"Verily, Sadaqat is in the cause of Allah,"

then the scholars would have explained the cause, and would have generalized it to the mentioned categories, and all other good causes.

Note: The *Prophet* said,

"Charity given to a poor is one charity, but charity given to a poor relative is two charities (double reward)."

So, it is recommended to send your *Zakat* / *Sadaqat* to your poor relatives wherever they may live.

ZAKAT-ABLE ITEMS

Gold	$ 0
Silver	$ 0
Cash on hand	$ 0
Checking Account	$ 0
Savings Account	$ 0
Business Bank Account(s)	$ 0
Stocks	$ 0
Business Merchandise Inventory	$ 0
Retirement Plans (401K/IRA/etc.)	$ 0
Accounts Receivable	$ 0
Total:	$ 0

BOOKS BY *QAZI FAZL ULLAH*

Qazi Fazl Ullah has written other books. Below is a short list with summaries.

FIQH KEE TAREEKH WA IRTIQA *(URDU)*

Islam is *Deen* (religion) and is a complete code of life. Its laws are of two types, textual and deduced, but how the text is interpreted and how laws are deduced therefrom is called *"Jurisprudence"* and the laws are called *Fiqh,* and how this *Fiqh* got developed and compiled. This book gives the details about its stages of development.

MOHAMMADUR RASOOLULLAH *(URDU)*

The biography of the *Prophet Muhammad* was preserved from day one by his blessed companions. Then scholars and historians have written books in this regard in different times, both concise and detailed. This book on the biography of *Prophet Muhammad* is an excellent balance of concise and detailed, as a concise a book sometimes misses things and people do not have time to read and understand too detailed a book. Another important feature of this book is that almost with every important part of the *Prophet's* biography, the relevant part of the *Holy Quran* has been quoted, which illustrates that the *Prophet's* life was the practical shape of the *Holy Book*.

SARMAYA DARANA NIZAM ISHTIRAKIYAT AUR ISLAM (URDU)

Humans, throughout their history, have thought ahead and planned their economics and economical needs. They created systems for these purposes. The three systems most widely practiced in history are capitalism, communism, and *Islam*. This book is a comparative study of these 3 economical systems and it proves that the *Islamic* system bestowed upon us by the Creator is the best one with regard to justice and no room for exploitation.

DAWAT O JIHAD (URDU)

The basic duty of every *Prophet* and his followers was and is to call the people towards *Allah* in a peaceful, attractive, and convincing way, and wherever and whenever they encountered resistance and hindrances in this regard, they must remove these hindrances. At times, this leads to fights, as when the conspiracy is big and the opponents try to take away their fundamental rights, so they have the right to defend it but how, when, and where? In this book, it is mentioned that *Islam* teaches us to convey, convince, and convert, but not to coerce. This book is an answer to anti-*Islamic* propaganda, especially about the concept of *Jihad* in *Islam*.

ISLAM AUR SIYASAT (URDU)

Islam and Politics—as it is known from the title that this book discusses *Islamic* political system, because *Islam* is *Deen*, meaning a complete code of life and not a set of a few rituals. It has its own system for state and government. So, wherever *Muslims* are in power, if they will implement this system, they meet the needs of everyone, regardless of color, caste, or religion. *Islam* covers the details, such as how to elect a government, and how to run the state to provide peace and justice to all.

RIYASATI ISLAMI KA TASWWAR (URDU)

The title means the concept of an *Islamic* state, and *"concept"* means its conduct. In this book, it is mentioned how and why a state and government is needed, and how that state and government may be and should be run. The Creator *Allah* the Almighty knows all our needs, necessities, qualities and shortcomings, so the system he has given is the only system that can ensure people's security and safety and can provide them peace and justice, making the state a welfare state.

USOOLUT - TAFSEER (ARABIC)

Every branch of science has its own rules, principles and methodologies, which provide guidelines for explaining it and how to interpret it, so this methodology is a circle or limits one may keep himself confines to so he will not get lost or go astray.

This book covers the explanation of the *Holy Quran*, the last and final book of *Allah*. The book of *Allah* is the basic source of *Islam* and *Islamic* law, so its explanation requires certain rules to be followed in its explanation, so one may not be unbridled and without restraint, otherwise he will put his faith in danger.

DIRAYATUR RIWAYAH (ARABIC)

Hadith (sayings, actions and sanctions) of *Prophet Muhammad* is the second fundamental source of *Islam* and *Islamic* laws and also it is the interpretation of the *Holy Quran*. The companions of the *Prophet Muhammad* have preserved them in their memories and in their scriptures and the second and third generation took it from them and preserved them as well. Later on, when there was a fear of perversion, then these *Ahadith* were compiled officially and later on, the authentic scholars gathered them together in various books. Furthermore, critics compiled a biography of all these narrators and put certain rules about how a *Hadith* could be accepted. This book includes all these details.

HUJJIYATI HADITH (URDU)

This book is regarding the authenticity of *Hadith* of the *Prophet*, as there is a baseless propaganda that *Hadith* were not written in the time of the *Prophet*, but later on, making them unreliable. This is wrong, as *Sahaba* used to write *Ahadith* and sometimes the *Prophet* himself used to order them to write. But they trusted their memory more than writing. Official compilation took place later on, when *Muslim* rulers became aware of the weakness of people's memories and the loss of those individuals writing. This book provides all these details and makes it clear that *Hadith* is *Wahi* (Revelation) and source of *Islamic Shariah* (Law).

FUNDAMENTALISM, SECULARISM AUR ISLAM (URDU)

Propaganda is being spread either because of ignorance or with mala fide intention that *Islam* is fundamentalism.

Fundamentalism was a term used for Christianity when it blocked the ways of scientific research, invention and development, and some people wanted to adopt it as a basic guideline for states and government. So those who were with research and development branded that as fundamentalism. But *Islam* does not stop or block progress and research; rather, it encourages it and even orders scholars to go ahead and do research, as discussed in this book.

AL IJTIHADU WAT TAQLEED (URDU)

Humans are social and intellectual animals. They have all the same needs as animals, but they are distinct from them because of their intellect as they are looking for their ease, to do a little and get a lot. For this purpose, some intellectuals invent things and others follow them. Then as they are bound to obey the *Deen* of *Allah*, there are other intellectuals who deduce laws from its fundamental sources: the *Quran* and the *Sunnah*, and the less intellectuals follow them, as they should. This is the only intellectual and reasonable way. This book explains this issue and its importance.

<u>MUSALMAN AURAT</u> *(URDU)*

Allah created the world. He created humans and made them men and women. He gave different qualities to both genders for the smooth running of this life to depend upon each other, but as humans they are equal. Some women made history and they did memorable work that many men could not have done. This small book mentions some of the great work of some great women, particularly *Muslim* women, to make it clear that *Islam* deeply respects women and appreciates their contributions to society.

<u>ASMATI RASOOL OR ZAWAJI AAISHA</u> *(URDU)*

This world is a combination of opposites and some people have been given a great status. The messengers of *Allah* are the chosen and beloved of *Allah*. He made them and built them up for himself and his work. They are the most respected and honored people, and they must be given respect, as any disgrace to them can harm the feelings and sentiments of their followers, which can cause trouble. In this book this issue is discussed, as well as a misconception about the *Prophet's* marriage to *Aaisha*; namely, that she was minor at that time. Academically and research fully, this book corrects this misconception.

AL FARA'ID FIL AQA'ID (ARABIC)

Aqeedah and *Aqa'id* means faith and beliefs, respectively, and they are the base of *Deen*. Certain beliefs are the contents of *Iman*. What is important for a *Muslim* to believe? These are detailed in this concise book. Some *Muslim* sects have misconstrued some of these beliefs, so the book mentions that as well and makes the right faith clear.

QAWA'IDUT - TAJWEED (ARABIC)

One of the basic duties of the *Prophet* was to teach his followers how to recite the holy book properly. His *Sahabah* learnt it from him and then this became a specific science in future generations. They not only taught their students the proper way of recitation, they also wrote books about it. This science is called *Tajweed*, which literally means to make good, but in this science, it means to recite good. This book prescribes the basic rules for *Tajweed* as proper pronunciation not only makes the words and sounds good but also helps in giving the proper meaning of the word.

AL QAWA'IDUL FIQHIYAH (ARABIC)

Islam is *Deen* and a complete system and code of life. For each and every aspect of life there are rules and laws in *Islam*. Some of these rules are in text of the *Quran* and the *Sunnah*, while some others are deduced therefrom. For deduction, the authentic jurists have laid down rules of deduction and the qualities required for themselves. Then, after deduction, they have found some commonalities in different laws in different chapters, so they laid down a common rule for that and these rules called *Al Qawa'idul - Fiqhiyah*, or legal maxims, which make the study of *Fiqh* easy and understandable. This book includes some known and famous legal maxims in all four schools of jurisprudence.

AL JIHAD FIL ISLAM (ARABIC)

Jihad is a very important issue in *Islam*; to defend life, property, honor and faith is not only a well-known right in each and every culture but also a duty in *Islam*, but how and when? This book is written on this subject. As this issue is quite controversial, this is a reasonable answer to these questions in the light of the *Quran* and *Sunnah*.

MAULANA UBAIDULLAH SINDHI (URDU)

Maulana Ubaidullah Sindhi, originally from a *Sikh* family, accepted *Islam* when he was a teenager. He studied *Deen* in the proper and traditional way, then joined the freedom movement. He went through a lot of difficulties, and lived in exile for 24 years. As a revolutionary leader, he is controversial and many people wrote against him as well as for him. This book describes his personality, struggle, and thoughts to know who he was and how he was.

ASMATI RASOOL AND KHATMI NUBUWWAT (URDU)

Asmati Rasool and *Khatmi Nubuwwat* are reasonable and logical. This book consists of two parts. The defense of the *Prophet* and that of him being the last and final *Prophet* of *Allah* is a reasonable and logical thing, as *Allah* sent messengers in different times to different areas and different nations, and when they worked in their respected times in those areas, *Allah* sent the *Prophet Muhammad* to the entire world to combine their work and bring humanity together on the same theme, subject and faith that all those earlier messengers were sent for. This book is a concise, detailed and logical interpretation of this finality.

SAYYIDAH AAISHA'S AGE AT MARRIAGE (ENGLISH)

Islam is a Natural *Deen* or *Deen* of Nature. This is a balanced *Deen* providing a comprehensive justice system, and the *Holy Prophet* is the perfect role model as a perfect human. His words, actions, and sanctions are the proper interpretation of the *Holy Quran* and the second fundamental source of laws in *Islam*. There is a commonly held belief, especially among critics of *Islam*, that the *Prophet* married *Aaisha* when she was only nine years of age. In this book, all the details about this issue is given that how this word *Tis'aa* (which means nine) happened there and what the real story is to counter the false accounts and correct the record.

JIHAD IN ISLAM : WHY, HOW, AND WHEN?

(ENGLISH)

Jihad as a word in *Arabic* means struggle or striving hard, especially for a noble cause, while as a term in *Islam*, it specifically means to fight in the path/cause of *Allah*. But when does this fight happen? When it is inevitable and unavoidable as the very integrity of a state, the lives of its citizens or the very ideology is facing a big danger. But a very baseless smear campaign is going on against *Jihad* and it is branded as a synonym to terrorism, so this book is a must to make the true concept of *Jihad* clear and counter the propaganda.

SHARIA AND POLITICS (ENGLISH)

Islam is *Deen* and *Deen* means a complete system and a perfect code of life as this is given by the very creator of the worlds, who knows all about his creatures, their qualities and their shortcomings, and can provide a perfect solution to their problems. But unfortunately, some people have been doing wrong in the name of *Khalafat* and presenting their wrong idea as the *Islamic* political system, so there was great need of a book that can present the proper shape of an *Islamic* state and *Islamic* political system given by the Creator; when executed properly, it is actually a mercy and blessing for the creatures. This book explains this concept clearly.

HAJJ & UMRAH IN ALL FOUR SCHOOLS OF JURISPRUDENCE (ENGLISH)

Hajj (pilgrimage to *Mecca*) is one of the Five Pillars of *Islam* and a very important but a complicated type of *Ibadah* (worship) as *Muslims* from all around the world get together to perform it together. They follow the interpretation of their *Imams* (jurists), so sometimes they look at others when they do not perform a specific virtue the way they do, then they think they are doing wrong, which is not so, but all of them are performing correctly according to the interpretation of their *Imams*. This book gives all these details in sequence according to all four *Imams* the *Muslim Ummah* follows.

MOON SIGHTING, SALATUL TARAWEEH AND SALATUL WITR (ENGLISH)

The *Islamic* Calendar is lunar-based. Its different *Ibadaat* time is based on moon-sighting; the lunar month starts with the new moon. Even though astronomy tells us what day the moon will be born (i.e., new) with perfect accuracy, discerning on which day it will be visible in a specific area is still not accurate. That is why differences in opinion happen all over the world, and should we to go by the calendar or by a sighting?

Also, at *Ramadan*, which is the most important month in *Islam* as a mandatory *Ibadah*, fasting is mandatory as well, but there is an extra, highly recommended *Ibadah,* the *Taraweeh*, but how many *Rakat* should we pray? *Muslims* differ about this. Another important *Ibadah* is *Salat Ul Witr*. We use this prayer all year, but during *Ramadan* this is prayed in *Jama'at* and different *Imams* have different opinions regarding the number of *Rakats* and its procedure. So, this book gives all the details about these three important issues.

SCIENCE OF HADITH (ENGLISH)

Hadith is the second fundamental source of *Islamic* law. They are the words, actions and sanctions of the *Holy Prophet*. To record all these in memory and writing, to compile it and to record the biography of those narrators who did this great job and this is considered as a miracle of the *Prophet*. But the enemies of *Islam* used to create doubts in this regard. This book is written on this subject, and it is enough an answer to all the objections that people made from different angles.

ABOUT THE AUTHOR

Qazi Fazl Ullah is an American philosopher, linguist, and author. He is *Fazil Wafaqul Madaris* where he studied *Arabic* grammar, *Arabic* literature, *Fiqh*, jurisprudence, logic, philosophy, *Ilmul Kalam, Seerah, Tafseer, Hadith,* and *Islamic* history. He studied at *Peshawar University* and *Islamic University Islamabad* in *Pakistan* and specialized in law, economics, and political science. He has taught all these subjects in *Pakistan* and the United States at different institutions. He was elected as a *National Assembly Parliamentarian* in *Pakistan*. He worked in underserved areas to provide jobs, build infrastructure, schools, museums, public health facilities, and increase communication technologies as the chair of the *Social Action Board*. He has traveled extensively throughout the Middle East, North Africa, Europe, South East Asia, North and Central America. He has given seminars in various parts of the world in these subjects. He speaks and has given lectures and seminars in *Urdu, Pashto, Farsi,* English, and *Arabic*. He has published works in *Pashto, Urdu, Arabic,* and English internationally. He has given the complete *Tafsir Ul Quran* in *Pashto* multiple times in *Pakistan*. He has also given *Tafsir Ul Quran* in *Urdu, Pashto,* and English in the United States. It includes *Usul Ul Fiqh, Usul Ul Mirath, Hadith al Qudsi, Hadith an Nabawi* in English on multiple occasions. He considers himself a student to continue acquisitions of knowledge. He is currently leading *Tafsir Ul Quran, Usual Al Fiqh, Seerat Un Nabi,* Science of Inheritance (*Mirath*) in English and *Al Mukhtar Lil Fatawa, Dirayat Ul Riwaya* in *Arabic* in Los Angeles, California.

www.ingramcontent.com/pod-product-compliance
Lightning Source LLC
Chambersburg PA
CBHW031148160426
43193CB00008B/293